THE AMERICAN PEOPLE

O *The Native American People of the East*

● *The Native American People of the West*

O *The American People in Colonial New England*

O *The American People in the Colonial South*

O *The American People in the Antebellum North*

O *The American People in the Antebellum South*

O *The American People on the Western Frontier*

O *The American People in the Industrial City*

O *The American People in the Depression*

O *The American People in the Age of Kennedy*

The Native American People Of the West

Edited by
P. RICHARD METCALF

James Axtell, Series Editor

Pendulum Press, Inc.   West Haven, Connecticut

Clothbound Edition ISBN 0-88301-082-8 Complete Set
0-88301-084-4 This Volume

Paperback Edition ISBN 0-88301-066-6 Complete Set
0-88301-068-2 This Volume

Library of Congress Catalog Card Number 72-95876

Published by
Pendulum Press, Inc.
The Academic Building
Saw Mill Road
West Haven, Connecticut 06516

Printed in the United States of America

Cover Design by Dick Brassil, Silverman Design Group
Cover Print Courtesy The Bettmann Archive

CONTENTS

ABOUT THE EDITOR

P. Richard Metcalf graduated *magna cum laude* from Northwestern University, received an M.A. degree from Yale University and is currently completing the requirements for a Ph.D. at Yale. He is also on the faculty there as an instructor in history and American Studies, teaching a seminar on Indian history and customs. Mr. Metcalf has contributed numerous articles to a forthcoming volume, *Encyclopedia of the West.*

ABOUT THE SERIES EDITOR

James Axtell, the recipient of a B.A. degree from Yale University and a Ph.D. from Cambridge University, has also studied at Oxford University and was a postdoctoral fellow at Harvard University. Mr. Axtell has taught history at Yale and is currently Associate Professor of Anglo-American History at Sarah Lawrence College. He is on the editorial board of *History of Education Quarterly* and has been a consultant to the American Council of Learned Societies. He has published several articles and reviews and is the author of a forthcoming book, *The School upon a Hill: Education and Society in Colonial New England.*

ACKNOWLEDGMENTS

Grateful acknowledgment is made to the authors and publishers who granted permission to reprint the following selections:

American Indian Life, by Elsie Clews Parsons, reprinted by permission of University of Nebraska Press.

An Apache Life-Way, by Morris E. Opler, reprinted by permission of the author and University of Chicago Press.

Black Elk Speaks, by John G. Niehardt, reprinted by permission of University of Nebraska Press.

The Cheyenne Indians, by George B. Grinnell, reprinted by permission of Yale University Press.

Childhood and Youth in Jicarilla Apache Society, by Morris E. Opler, reprinted by permission of the author and University of Chicago Press.

"Crime and Punishment in Tlingit Society," by Kalervo Oberg, reproduced by permission of the American Anthropological Association from the *American Anthropoligist,* vol. 36, no. 2, 1934.

Five Indian Tribes of the Upper Missouri, by Edwin T. Denig, reprinted by permission of University of Oklahoma Press.

Hopi Ethics, by Richard D. Brandt, reprinted by permission of University of Chicago Press.

Ojibwa Woman, by Ruth Landes, reprinted by permission of Columbia University Press.

Potlatch and Totem and the Recollections of an Indian Agent, by William M. Halliday, reprinted by permission of J.M. Dent and Sons Ltd.

The Sacred Pipe: Black Elk's Account of the Seven Rites of the Oglala Sioux, by Joseph E. Brown, reprinted by permission of University of Nebraska Press.

Tabeau's Narrative of the Loisel's Expedition to the Upper Missouri, by Annie H. Abel, reprinted by permission of University of Oklahoma Press.

FOREWORD

The American People is founded on the belief that the study of history in the schools and junior levels of college generally begins at the wrong end. It usually begins with abstract and pre-digested *conclusions*—the conclusions of other historians as filtered through the pen of a textbook writer—and not with the primary sources of the past and unanswered *questions*—the starting place of the historian himself.

Since we all need, use, and think about the past in our daily lives, we are all historians. The question is whether we can be skillful, accurate, and useful historians. The only way to become such is to exercise our historical skills and interests until we gain competence. But we have to exercise them in the same ways the best historians do or we will be kidding ourselves that we are *doing* history when in fact we are only absorbing sponge-like the results of someone else's historical competence.

Historical competence must begin with one crucial skill—the ability to distinguish between past and present. Without a sharp sense of the past as a different time from our own, we will be unable to accord the people of the past the respect that we would like to receive from the people of the future. And without according them that respect, we will be unable to recognize their integrity as individuals or to understand them as human beings.

A good sense of the past depends primarily on a good sense of the present, on experience, and on the imaginative empathy to relate ourselves to human situations not our own. Although most students have had a relatively brief experience of life and have not yet given full expression to their imaginative sympathies, they do possess the one essential prerequisite for the study of history—the lives they have lived from birth to young adulthood. This should be the initial focus of their study of the past, not remotely adult experiences to which they cannot yet relate, such as politics, diplomacy, and war.

Thus the organizing perspective of this series is the universal life experiences that all people have: being born, growing up, loving and marrying, working and playing, behaving and misbehaving, worshipping, and dying. As only he could, Shakespeare portrayed these cycles in *As You Like It* (Act II, scene vii):

> All the world's a stage,
> And all the men and women merely players.
> They have their exits and their entrances;
> And one man in his time plays many parts,
> His acts being seven ages. At first the infant,
> Mewling and puking in the nurse's arms.
> And then the whining school-boy, with his satchel
> And shining morning face, creeping like snail
> Unwillingly to school. And then the lover,
> Sighing like furnace, with a woeful ballad
> Made to his mistress' eyebrow. Then a soldier,
> Full of strange oaths, and bearded like a pard;
> Jealous in honour, sudden and quick in quarrel,
> Seeking the bubble reputation
> Even in the cannon's mouth. And then the justice,
> In fair round belly with good capon lined,
> With eyes severe and beard of formal cut,
> Full of wise saws and modern instances;
> And so he plays his part. The sixth age shifts
> Into the lean and slipper'd pantaloon,
> With spectacles on nose and pouch on side;
> His youthful hose, well saved, a world too wide
> For his shrunk shank; and his big manly voice,
> Turning again toward childish treble, pipes
> And whistles in his sound. Last scene of all,
> That ends this strange eventful history,

> Is second childishness, and mere oblivion,
> Sans teeth, sans eyes, sans taste, sans everything.

These are experiences to which any student can relate and from which he can learn, simply because they surround him daily in his home, community, and not least, school.

There is an additional reason for focussing on the universal life cycle. If history is everything that happened in the past, obviously some things were and are more important than others. Until fairly recently the things historians have found important have been the turning points or *changes* in history—"great" men and "great" events. But recently, with the help of anthropologists, historians have come to a greater awareness of the importance of stability and inertia, of *non*-change in society. For every society—and therefore its history—is a mixture of change and stability, of generally long periods of fixity punctuated now and then by moments of modification and change.

The major reason for the stability of society is the conservative bent of human behavior and ideals, the desire to preserve, hold, fix, and keep stable. People acquire habits and habits impede change. The habits people acquire are the common ways the members of a society react to the world—how they behave and feel and think in common—which distinguish them from other societies and cultures. So at bottom history is about ordinary people, how they did things alike and together that gave continuity and durability to their society so that it could change to meet new circumstances without completely losing its former identity and character.

America is such a society and *The American People* is an attempt to provide representative selections from primary sources about the lives and habits of ordinary people in periods of history that are usually known in textbooks for their great changes.

Since the experience of each student is the only prerequisite for the study of primary sources at the first level, annotations and introductory material have been reduced to a minimum, simply enough to identify the sources, their authors, and the circumstances in which they were written.

But the remains of the past are mute by themselves. Many sources have survived that can tell us what happened in the past and why, but they have to be questioned properly to reveal their secrets. So by way of illustration, a number of questions have been asked in each chapter, but these should be supplemented by the students whose experiences and knowledge and interests are, after all, the flywheel of the educational process. Although the questions and sources are divided into chapters, they should be used freely in the other chapters; the collection should be treated as a whole. And although most of the illustrative questions are confined to the sources at hand, questions that extend to the present should be asked to anchor the acquired knowledge of the past in the immediate experience of the present. Only then will learning be real and lasting and history brought to life.

INTRODUCTION

There were many different ways of life among the native American people of the West. Near the upper Great Lakes, the Ojibwa lived in bark lodges and gathered wild rice in their bark canoes. On the plains, the nomadic, tepee-dwelling Sioux and Cheyenne followed the seasonal migrations of the buffalo herds. In the arid Southwest, the Pueblo peoples constructed apartment cities of the adobe brick and cultivated irrigated fields. And in the Pacific Northwest, the Tlingit ocean seafarers sailed beyond sight of land to hunt whales in seventy-foot canoes and lived in great houses of sawn planks. To further complicate matters, there were more different languages spoken by western Indians than by the peoples of Europe and Asia combined, and the physical appearance of Indians varied almost as greatly. And yet there were many over-all similarities which make it possible to discuss them as a recognizably distinct group in the history of the American people. Most importantly, the Indians lived in a world without science, technology, or industry as we know it. The populations of their societies were small by our standards, and their survival was dependent on unpredictable natural forces largely beyond their control. Accordingly, Indian life was incorporated into the cycles of the natural environment in a way quite different from the experience of modern white Americans.

The very factors which made the western Indians distinct also make it difficult to study their history and customs. Because the Indians possessed no written language, the student must rely for source materials largely upon what white observers have said about them. This material can be divided into three types: (1) historical observations left by white explorers, traders, and travelers who visited Indian societies before the onslaught of massive white encroachment; (2) the scholarly observations of anthropologists who have made a directed effort to study and understand Indian life before it completely disappears; and (3) statements made by Indians directly to white men and recorded more or less verbatim. This book contains source material of all three types so as to enable the student to determine for himself what kinds are the most reliable and impartial. Aspects of most major western Indian life-ways are illustrated in the documents, providing a means to discover both the similarities and varieties among Indian societies.

I. BIRTH

Childbirth was, as in most societies, an important event for the Indians. Every effort was made to insure the health and safety of the mother and child. What were some of the precautions taken before birth? After birth? Why? How much did the Indian mother know about having babies before she became pregnant? How did she learn it? How were pregnant women regarded? How were new mothers? Who took care of the mother and baby during and after birth? What was the significance of the pre-partum rituals? What was the function of the cradle-board? How were infants treated? Why? Did the Indians practice birth-control?

Waiyautitsa of the Zuñi

The Zuñi Indians of New Mexico have managed to preserve their traditional way of life right into the present day. The woman in this selection lived about 1900, and her biography was written by Elsie C. Parsons, an anthropologist and member of the Zuñi tribe. (E. C. Parsons, ed., American Indian Life *(1922), 167-69.)*

Courtship past for the time being, courtship by magic or otherwise, Waiyautitsa is now, let us say, an expectant mother. Her household duties continue to be about the same, but certain precautions, if she inclines to be very circumspect, she does take. She will not test the heat of her oven by sprinkling it in the usual way with bran, for if she does, her child, she has heard, may be born with a skin eruption. Nor will she look at a corpse or help dress a dead animal lest her child be born dead or disfigured. She has heard that, even as a little girl if she ate the whitish leaf of the corn husk, her child would be an albino. If her husband eats this during the pregnancy, the result would be the same. On her husband fall a number of other pregnancy tabus, perhaps as many as fall on her, if not more. If he hunts and maims an animal, the child will be similarly maimed—deformed or perhaps blind. If he joins in a masked dance, the child may have some mask-suggested misshape or some eruption like the paint on the mask. If he sings a great deal, the child will be a cry-baby.

Perhaps Waiyautitsa has wished to determine the sex of the child. In that case she may have made a pilgrimage with a rain priest to Corn Mesa to plant a prayer stick which has to be cut and painted in one way for a boy, in another way for a girl. (Throughout the Southwest blue or turquoise is associated with maleness, and yellow with femaleness.) Wanting a girl—and girls are wanted in Zuñi quite as much as boys, if not more—Waiyautitsa need not make the trip to the mesa; instead her husband may bring her to wear in her belt scrapings from a stone in a phallic shrine near the mesa. When labor sets in and the pains are slight, indicating, women think, a girl, Waiyautitsa may be told by her mother, "Don't sleep, or you will have a boy." A nap during labor effects a change of sex. When the child is about to be born, Waiyautitsa is careful, too, if she wants a girl, to see that the custom of sending the men out of the house at this time is strictly observed.

After the birth, Waiyautitsa will lie in for several days, four, eight, ten or twelve, according to the custom of her family. Whatever the custom, if she does not observe it, she runs the risk of "drying up" and dying. She lies on a bed of sand heated by hot stones, and upon her abdomen is placed a hot stone. Thus is she "cooked," people say, and creatures whose mothers are not thus treated are called un-cooked, raw—they are the animals, the gods, Whites. To be "cooked" seems to be tantamount in Zuñi to being human.

It is the duty of Waiyautitsa's mother-in-law, the child's paternal grandmother, to look after mother and child during the confinement, and at its close to carry the child outdoors at dawn and present him or her to the Sun. Had Waiyautitsa lost children, she might have invited a propitious friend, some woman who had had many children and lost none, to attend the birth and be the first to pick up the child and blow into his mouth. In these circumstances the woman's husband would become the initiator of the child, if a boy, when the child was to be taken into the Kachina society. Generally the child's father chooses some man from the house of his own kuku or paternal aunt to be the initiator or godfather, so to speak, of the child. Ceremonial rites usually fall to the paternal relatives.

But the infant will receive attentions of a ritual or magical nature, likewise from his mother and her household. He is placed on a cradle board in which, near the position of his heart, a bit of turquoise is inlaid to preclude the cradle bringing any harm to its tenant. Left alone, a baby runs great risk—some family ghost may come and hold him, causing him to die within four days. And so a quasi-fetichistic ear of corn, a double ear thought of as mother and child, is left alongside the baby as a protector. That the baby may teethe promptly, his gums may be rubbed by one who has been bitten by a snake—"snakes want to bite." To make the child's hair grow long and thick, his grandfather or uncle may puff the smoke of native tobacco on his head. That the child may not be afraid in the dark, water-soaked embers are rubbed over his heart the first time he is taken out at night—judging from what I have seen of Zuñi children and adults a quite ineffectual method. That the child may keep well and walk early, hairs from a deer are burned, and the child held over the smoke—deer are never sick, and rapid is their gait. Their hearing, too, is acute, so discharge from a deer's ear will be put into the baby's ear. That the child may talk well and with tongues, the tongue of a snared mocking bird may be cut out and held to the baby to lick. The bird will then be released in order that, as it regains its tongue and "talks," the child will talk. A youth who speaks in addition to his native tongue Keresan, English and Spanish, has been pointed out to me as one who had licked mocking bird tongue.

A Fox Indian Woman

The Fox Indians lived around the Mississippi River in the region where Iowa, Wisconsin, and Illinois meet. This selection is from the verbal autobiography of a Fox woman about fifty years old, taken down in 1918. (Truman Michelson, "Autobiography of a Fox Indian Woman," Bureau of American Ethnology Annual Report, XL (1925), 315-21.)

And when I had been living with him for half a year, soon I ceased having catamenial flows. Thereupon I was given instructions again, "Well, this is what has happened: probably you are to have a child. When anything is cooked and it is burned, it must not be eaten so that the children's afterbirths will not adhere. And nuts are not to be eaten, so that the babies will be able to break through the caul. And in winter, one is not to warm their feet, so that the babies will not adhere (to the caul). And (women) are not to join their feet to those of their husbands, so that (the babies) will not be born feet-first. And the feet of no (animals) are to be eaten. And one must be careful not to touch crawfish. Also, if these are touched when one is enceinte, the babies will be born feet-first. It is said that (women) have a hard time when they are born that way. That is why one believes and fears (what one has been told), so that one will not suffer a long time at childbirth. It is better to do what we are told. And no corpse is to be touched. If it is touched the babies would die after they are born, by inheriting it. And if the dead are looked at, they are to be looked at with straight eyes. Also it is said that if they are looked at slantingly, the babies will be cross-eyed. And if cranes are touched, the babies will always look upward. The children will not be able to look upon the ground. And when any one drowns, if he is touched, the babies would die. These are the number of things one is forbidden to do. And it is told that one should carry wood always on one's back so that the babies will be loosened (i.e., born easily). Again, after (a woman) knows that she is pregnant, she is to cease to have anything to do with her husband. (Otherwise) the babies will be filthy when they are born. When their parents do not observe this, (the babies) begin to move around. That is the rule when that happens. For we women have a hard time at childbirth. We suffer. Some are killed by the babies. But we are not afraid of it, as we have been made to be that way. That is probably the reason why we are not afraid of it. Oh, if we were all afraid of it, when we all became old, that is as far as we could go. We should not be able to branch out (to a new generation). So at childbirth we should do only what we are told. The ones who do not do as they are told are the ones who are injured by their children.''

I have now told you all how it is, though I did not know about this, namely, how hard childbirth is. Even at this time I was not able to know about it. Only after I had given birth (to a child) would I know how hard it is. Soon surely my abdomen grew large. I was ashamed. When there was a dance I did not go there as I was ashamed.

Soon after eight months were by, my mother-in-law came. She came of talk with my mother. ''Now is the time when she is on the point of giving birth (to a child). We should build (a little wickiup) beforehand for her so that she may be delivered there. That is why I took my time coming, (thinking) she might be sick at night,'' she said to my mother. They built it. After they built it, she said to my mother, ''Well, you may summon me whenever she is sick.''

Soon I became sick in the evening when lying alone. I did not tell of it. Soon I was told, ''You might be sick?'' ''Yes,'' I answered, ''I am sick and have a little pain in the small of my back,'' I said to my mother. ''Oh ho,'' she said, ''very likely now is the time when you are to have a child. I shall summon her. For she said, 'you will summon me.' '' In a little after she came, she said to me, ''Come, go to the little wickiup.'' (Blankets) were spread for me. When I sat down comfortably a strap was fastened from above. ''You are to hold on to this when you begin to feel intense pain,'' I was told. I then felt more intense pain. After a while I was told, ''Lie down. When you begin to suffer acute pain you are to try to sit up. You are to sit on your knees and you are to sit erect.'' I did so. I would hold on to the strap. (The child) could not be born.

After midnight I was nearly unable to get up. The women who were attending me became frightened. Then they said among themselves, ''We shall pray (for help).'' My mother-in-law took Indian tobacco and went to a women skilled in obstetrics for help. And when that woman came, she at once boiled some medicine. After she had boiled it, she said: ''Let her in any case sit up for a while. You must hold her so that she will not fall over.'' After I was made to sit up, she spat upon my head; and she gave me (the medicine) to drink. After she had given me (the medicine) to drink, she began singing. She started to go out singing and went around the little wickiup singing. When she danced by where I was, she knocked on the side. ''Come out if you are a boy,'' she would say. And she would again begin singing. When she danced by she again knocked the side. "Come out if you are a girl," she would say again. After she sang four times in a circle, she entered (the wickiup). And she gave me (medicine) to drink. "Now it will be born. She may lie down. Only lay her down carefully. You must hold her knees straight up," she said. Lo, sure enough, a little boy was born.

Then I knew how painful childbirth was. After I had borne (the child) I was not in pain in any spot. I was well. They cut off the baby's navel with one inch of the cord on it. A brand-new pair of scissors was used. They tied up the place where he was cut. His belly was washed. The next day he was placed in a cradle. And they tied a little piece of meat on his navel with a cloth going around (his body), tying it on his abdomen. "You must moisten him once in a while so that his umbilical cord will drop off soon." I was told. I did so to him. I did not wash him myself. My mother attended to him for me. In three days his umbilical cord dropped off. He could not draw the milk out for two days when I nursed him.

Then, "You must always keep him in a cradle: (otherwise) he might have a long head, (or) he might be humpbacked, (or) he might be bow-legged. That is why they are placed carefully, so they will (not) be that way. When they are tied that way they will be straight. They are kept in cradles for nearly one year. Again, they are not to be held all the time. They are placed in a swing after they suckle so that they will not be a nuisance. They become trained to be left alone when one goes some place, if they are not cry-babies. And when they are constantly held some cry when they are laid down. (People) are bothered by them when they get them used to being constantly held," I was told.

I lived outside for thirty-three days.

Soon, when our little boy nearly knew how to talk, he became ill. I felt very sorrowful. Later on, indeed, he died. It is surely very hard to have death (in the family). One can not help feeling badly. "That is why I told you about it when you were both unfortunately frightening him," I was told. "That is why children are not struck. One would feel worse if one had beaten (the child)," I was told. I felt worse after he was buried. The fourth day we fed those who buried him in the evening. We began to make every kind of new finery. After we had made it, I began to think over the one whom we should adopt. I thought of all the babies. I found one as if this way: "This one perhaps is loved as much as I loved my baby," I thought. Then we adopted him, so that we in a way had a son.

Care of the Infant

The Jicarilla Apache Indians lived in northeastern New Mexico and southern Colorado. The following statements were made by Jicarilla informants to Morris Opler, an anthropologist who has spent his life studying the Apache. (M. E. Opler, Childhood and Youth in Jicarilla Apache Society *(1946), 14-24.)*

We don't allow a young baby's feet to be extended. We put grass or something soft under its knees until its navel is healed, for otherwise the navel won't heal properly. There is too much strain there if the feet are extended. And when carrying a young baby, you should always have a hide against its back and up over its neck to support its head so it won't wobble around.

The baby was always laid on a saddle blanket. They made their own saddle blankets in those days, of skin with the hair on. We don't cover the baby with the saddle blanket; we just put the baby on top of it. This is so the baby won't get sores at the navel, under the armpits, or at any of the soft places. The idea is that the saddle blanket is used on the horse to prevent it from getting sores, and so it is used to keep the baby from getting sores too.

When the baby is small the mother never chews gum [pitch of the pine tree]. If she doesn't listen to what the old women tell her and continues to chew it, the mucus will harden and dry in the child's nose, and it will be clogged up all the time.

To cover the child and keep it warm we used a robe with fur on, and wrapped it around and around, for we had nothing like safety pins. The hide of the wildcat was often used, with the fur inside. Cougar skin is good for a child's robe too. The hands were held down at the sides by the robe. When a child is going to sleep we always tie its hands to its sides like this. Then the baby does not move its hands in its sleep, wake itself up, scare itself, and start crying. When the baby wakes and starts to cry, we untie the string, open the blanket, and let it loose. Later, if the baby gets tired and starts to cry, we say it is crying for the cover again and tie the baby up and put it to sleep. Sometimes the baby is crying for a bath. After the bath it stops crying.

Formerly deer skins were used for diapers. They had to be washed off all the time. Sometimes the hair was left on; sometimes it was removed. For powder for the baby, the outer bark of the pine was ground very fine and applied when dry. This is used when the baby's navel is sore too. Buffalo chips were burned and the ashes used as baby powder also. It was used for the same purpose unburned when it was good and dry.

Old women make the cradles. Or an old woman who knows how can show the mother how to do it, for the mother can do it for her own children. Men never do it. The cradle is made when the child is born. Then it dries for a month or two. By that time the baby's navel is healed, and it is all right for it to have the legs extended.

When you ask an old woman to make a baby cradle for you, you have to roll a cigarette and put it on her foot. She won't be convinced she should do it if you use only the word. Often it is the mother's mother who does it. If the grandmother does not do it, the father or mother of the woman who is having the child can ask anyone who knows how. The cradle is made big enough so that it will take care of the baby until it is ready to walk.

When the baby is put in the cradle for the first time, the old woman who made it uses pollen; she sprinkles the cradle with it. Then she motions toward the cradle with the baby and puts it in the fourth time. There are turkey claws and turkey bones on the cradle to protect the baby and keep it in good health. To make the cradle pretty, beads are sewed along the sides of the buckskin and at the top near the child's head. The child is kept in the cradle until it is ready to walk.

The cradle for the boy and the girl are the same. It is kept and used again if another child comes along. If the child lives you can't throw it away. After it has been used for four children it is taken and hung on the east side of a spruce tree. The four who use one cradle should be the children of one woman. A woman who does not want four or more children will not have such a cradle made. A woman who has less than four children but is past childbearing age or is sick and knows she cannot have more children, hangs the cradle to the east on a young spruce tree.

If a child dies while it is still using a cradle, the cradle is buried with that baby—thrown away. Sometimes at the death of the child, they hang the cradle up. The body of the baby is never hung up in it, but is buried separately. If a cradle is being used for the second time and the first child who used it dies, the cradle will be thrown away or hung up. It has a ghost connected with it and won't be kept.

When a woman has reared four children and hangs up the cradle, if she doesn't want any more children, she drinks some medicine, lest it hurt if she has any more. She figures she has had enough. Some women know about this and instruct the mothers.

The egg is used with the fat of the bird. Rub these on the baby and it will feel well and sleep well too. Also, the brain and the eye are put in water, and this liquid is rubbed on the leg joints of a little baby. Then the baby will walk quickly and run around a great deal.

Porcupine fat and red ochre are mixed and used to paint the children so they will not get sick, although much sickness is around. The porcupine eats only the bark of pine trees and he dwells in the open air. He never has any sickness. That is why he is used this way.

If a little child gets a sick stomach and fever from eating excrement of some kind when the parents are not looking, use beggar-ticks pounded with dirt from the hole of a prairie dog. Boil this and give the liquid to the child to drink.

If a child gets weak and dreamy, there is something wrong in its stomach. So we use the deer stomach. It is boiled in water, cut into small pieces, and given to the child. The soup in which it is cooked is drunk also. Others of the family partake, for it is good for general health. And deer stomach is good for diarrhea in young and old.

We are afraid of the poorwill and do not use it. If this bird comes around camp, we throw rocks at it and drive it away, for if there is a little baby there, this bird makes the head of the child hot with fever. If this bird sits on a tipi pole, it makes the children inside the tipi sick.

One man knew a ceremony against it. If anyone got sick from it, he would take a small pinon tree and use the branches in his ceremony, beating them, and singing. Then he would motion to the directions with the branches, driving the sickness away.

The cottontail rabbit has a white dot on the forehead. Put your finger in ashes and then on the dot, then on the forehead of a baby. Then the ghosts are afraid to trouble the baby, and the baby will not be afraid of the ghosts either.

While a woman is nursing one child, she is not supposed to have intercourse with her husband and have a second child. If a woman has one little baby, with about two teeth, which she is still feeding from the breast, and at the same time she is carrying a second child, the first child will be sick, starved, and ailing and crying all the time. It spoils the mother's milk, and the child has diarrhea all the time and even excretes blood.

Babies who grow up under such conditions are going to be weaklings. We call them by a word that means "weakling." This baby is not going to walk or talk as soon as it should. Even as a grown person he will be this way. When a person is sick all the time, and every time he tries to do something he gets sick and is not worth anything, he is called this.

There are some good remedies to help a child with this condition. The fat around the heart of the buffalo is always kept for the children. The meat from around the backbone of the buffalo is kept too. When a year-old child is sick because the mother has another child on the way, they feed it this.

Marrow from the long bones of elk and deer, mixed with the root of a plant called "medicine that makes one fat," is good too. This can be rubbed on the body of the child or put in water and given to him to drink. Or, to restore the appetite and make the child feel better, you can crush the shell of the dung beetle and mix it with a mountain plant called "medicines which carry each other about."

Sometimes the child is so ill that they have to have a ceremony at which it is painted all over with red ochre. This makes it well again.

To wean a child, a mother puts something sour on her nipples. The child is first given a little tender meat to eat. The old people try to get the child to take different foods. When the small children first smell elk meat, they don't like it and don't want to eat it. So the old people chew it first and give it that way to the children to begin with. When a child of about two years of age won't eat, they give it a little piece of the meat of the Western tanager raw. Then the appetite comes back.

Don't feed tongue to the young even if they want it, not before they can speak. It will make their tongues too big, and they won't speak well.

Sometimes a woman will feed a child for a longer time on purpose, so that her husband will not bother her. They say that this is bad for the child, who gets sluggish and fat in an unhealthy way.

A few days after birth the Jicarilla baby takes part in an important ceremony. What is its purpose? Do modern Americans have similar ceremonies?

There is a ceremony of the earth which is a long-life ceremony. Every child goes through this. The gods gave the people this ceremony in the beginning. It is handed down from old times through the tribe. This ceremony was given to the people when they were already on this earth, before Monster Slayer came, however, and before the monsters were killed. It was not needed for life in the underworld before the emergence, for down there, there was no sickness, no death, no need for a "long-life" ceremony like this. But the earth is dangerous and evil; and this takes the children to the puberty ceremony safely.

The name of the ceremony is "water has been put on top of his head." It always takes place the fourth day after birth. Even if the mother is not well enough to stand up for the ceremony, it has to go on. In that case she lies down. They get someone who knows the songs to sing them for the baby. My father and S— and my father-in-law know this ceremony; J— knows it too. The man is paid according to what the family wants to give him; no certain things have to be given.

The child has not been washed before: this is the first time since birth that water has touched it. They do not use the water from springs or lakes when they have this ceremony. They use the water from rivers. It has to be from the sacred male rivers, the Arkansas and Rio Grande, and the sacred female rivers, the Pecos and the Canadian. When they first get the water they offer sacred stones, such as turqoise and red beads, to the rivers. Water from at least one of the male rivers and one of the female rivers must be mixed together. The one who has charge and is going to sing gets the water.

The singer starts early, before the sun comes up. He puts the water in a clay bowl. He sprinkles pollen sunwise in the form of a sun on top of the water. Then he does the same with specular iron ore and he makes four rays of pollen and specular iron ore extending outward to the directions, beginning with the east. Then he brings grama grass and snakeweed. Grama grass is used by all the holy people, like the gods. It is leader for the growing things, for the plants. Snakeweed is another holy one that is much used in the ceremonies and therefore has its place here. The singer puts grama grass in the water with the top part up. Then he crushes the snakeweed and puts in pieces from the inside of the plant top.

He now starts to sing about the pollen and the specular iron ore. He sings for long life for the child. He sings of those four rivers, because those rivers have long life, and we people live by means of water. He is holding the naked child in his hands. He dips his right hand in the water and sprinkles water four times on the baby's right foot. Then he does it to the right hand of the child, to the right shoulder, then to the top of the head, to the left shoulder, to the left hand, and to the left foot.

Now he washes the feet of the child with the water and works right up the baby's body to the head. Next he sprinkles water on the baby's blanket and on what is prepared for the baby's diaper. Now he is finished with the water. It is thrown four times to the east and is not entirely emptied till the fourth time.

The mother comes forward. Her hair is unbraided and loose, for the mother's hair is kept loose from the time of the birth of the child until this ceremony, to signify her holiness. When a girl goes through her puberty rite, she has her hair down also. After this ceremony the mother can do her hair in braids again.

The singer cuts four strips of deer skin from an unblemished and tanned buck or doe skin, one which has not been shot with an arrow or a bullet and therefore has no holes or cuts in it. He ties the strips together, end to end, making one long strip. He paints it red with red ochre while he sings. He puts pollen and then specular iron ore on it four times from end to end. This string is called "spider's thread." He raises the string and motions with it as though stretching it out. He holds one end to the baby's chest and stretches out the other end, giving the baby long life. He is facing the east all the while. He presses the string against the baby's chest and then against its back. If the child is a boy, he ties a piece of turquoise to one end of the string now; if it is a girl, he uses a piece of abalone. Then he puts the string down on the baby's clothes which have been laid before him.

He starts now to paint the baby's face. He uses the palm of his hand and paints the entire face with red ochre. Then he paints the mother's face, and next the father's. If other children of the mother are present, or any other children or adults, the singer paints them too. After this, pollen is put on the baby's face and on the faces of the others in the same order. Then the same is done with specular iron ore. The man is singing all the time he is doing this.

When all are painted, he motions four times with the baby, and the fourth time hands it to the father saying, "This is your baby." The father receives the baby, motions four times to the mother, and gives the baby to her the fourth time.

At the end of the ceremony the singer ties the string around the baby. He begins at the top of the baby's body and spirals it down along the body. The stone or shell is at the top. This string is kept on the child all the time till he walks around. After that the mother keeps it with the umbilical cord. She is supposed to keep it all her life.

The whole ceremony is over before noon. Its length depends on how many songs the man sings and how he conducts it. After the ceremony, they eat; all the relatives and friends come in the morning and are fed. They don't stay all day, though.

Pima Nursery Tales

The Pima Indian homeland is in southern Arizona along the Mexican border. These stories were recorded by an anthropologist in 1901. What is the function of these nursery tales? What kinds of lessons do they teach? Do they remind you *of any stories you were told as a child? (Frank Russell,* The Pima Indians, *Bureau of American Ethnology* Annual Report, *XXVI (1908), 242-47.)*

THE FIVE LITTLE ORPHANS AND THEIR AUNT

Five little Indians (not Pimas) were once left orphans because their parents had been killed by Apaches, and they got their aunt (their mother's younger sister) to come and live with them. She had no man, and it was very hard for her to take care of them. One day the children all went away to hunt, and they were met by five little rabbits (cottontails) in the mountains. The oldest of the rabbits came running to the children and crying, "Don't shoot me; I have something to tell you." So the children stood still and the rabbit said, "The Apaches have come to your place and burned down all the houses; you had better go home now." But the children surrounded the rabbit and killed it with an arrow and took it home.

When they reached home, they saw their aunt lying outside the ki in the shade, and something bloody near her. The oldest boy said, "Just look what auntie has been doing! She's been eating our paint and poisoned herself." But it was blood they saw coming out of her mouth, for the Apaches had come and killed her. When they came closer, they saw that a bunch of her hair had been cut off, and she looked so unnatural in death that they thought it was somebody else, and that their aunt had gone away. They had never seen a dead person before. So they said, "Let us dig a big hole and make a fire all day long and put hot stones in it, for she has gone to the mountains to get some mescal." So they did, and waited all day long till sunset, when she usually came, but she did not come. Then they said, "She has gone far and has a heavy load and is waiting for us to come and help her; let us go." But the oldest boy said, "No, she will come anyway, she always does, even if she has a heavy load." So they waited till night, and gave her up, and went into the house to sleep; but they kept their sandals on, as the Pimas always did, so they could start off quickly if there were danger.

In their sleep they heard her coming in her sandals, groaning and murmuring, so they all got up and went outdoors. They heard her go and look into the fire pit, and then come and stand in their midst. One said, "I think it is a ghost;" so they turned to the right and ran around the ki, and she followed them around and around. Finally they all went inside, still pursued, and the children stood on each side of the door and turned into stone. And the woman went away.

COYOTE AND THE QUAILS

Once Coyote was sleeping very soundly and a great number of quails came along and cut pieces of fat meat out of him; then they went on. Just as they were cooking the meat Coyote overtook them and said, "Oh, where did you get that nice fat meat? Give me some." They gave him some, and after he had eaten all he wanted he went on. When he had gone a little way, the quails called after him, "Coyote, you ate your own meat."

"What did you say?"

"Oh, nothing; we heard something calling behind the mountains." Presently they called again, "Coyote, you ate your own meat."

"What?"

"Oh, nothing; we heard somebody pounding his grinding stone."

So Coyote went on; but finally he felt his loss, and then he knew what the quails meant. So he said he would eat them up, and turned around after them. The quails flew above ground, and Coyote ran under them. Finally the quails got tired, but Coyote did not, for he was angry and did not feel fatigue.

By and by they came to a hole, and one of the smartest quails picked a cholla cactus branch and pushed it into the hole, and they all ran in after it. Coyote dug out the hole, and when he came to the first quail he said, "Was it you that told me I ate my own meat?" "No," said the quail, so he let him go, and he flew away. The next one he asked the same question and received the same reply, and let him go; and so on till the last quail was gone, and he came to the cactus branch. This was so covered with feathers that it looked like a quail, and the Coyote asked it the same question. There was no answer, and Coyote said, "I know it was you, because you do not answer." So he bit into it very hard and it killed him.

THE WOMAN AND COYOTE

Once the river rose very high and spread over the land. An Indian woman was going along with tortillas in a basket on her head, and she waded in the water up to her waist.

Coyote was afraid of the water, so he was up in a cottonwood tree. When he saw the woman he said, "Oh, come to this tree and give me some of those nice tortillas."

"No," said the woman, "I can not give them to you; they are for somebody else."

"If you do not come here I will shoot you," said Coyote, for he was supposed to have a bow. So she came to the tree and said, "You must come down and get them, for I can not climb trees." Coyote came down as far as he dared, but he was afraid of the water. Then the woman said, "Just see how shallow it is, only up to my ankles." But she was standing on a big stump. Coyote looked and thought it was shallow, so he jumped down and was drowned. And the woman went on.

THE PIMA BOY AND THE APACHES

An old woman once lived with her grandson. The boy's father had been killed by the Apaches and his mother taken captive. They had treated the woman very badly and burned her arms with hot ashes and coals and made big scars. The boy had heard these stories about his mother.

The boy and the old woman had a very hard time getting along, and he used to go where certain persons were grinding corn and brush a few grains as they fell from the metate into his blanket and carry them home and the grandmother would make soup of them, and that was the way they lived. But by and by these people went away and when the boy went to get some corn there was none there and he had nothing to take home. The grandmother scolded him and told him to go back; and when he refused she whipped him. Then he said, "I know where my mother is, and I am going to her." The old woman said, "No, you must not; the Apaches will kill you." But he said, "I am going; my mother will not let them harm me." So he went. His grandmother trailed him to the mountains, and finally from the very highest peak she saw him going along toward the camp. She also saw his mother, her daughter-in-law, out alone gathering seeds. She recognized her at a distance by the shining of her scars. The old woman ran after the boy, but when she caught up with him he stepped aside and turned into a saguaro. Then after she had turned around and gone back he resumed his form and went on to his mother.

When she saw him she cried out, "Don't come near me, the Apaches will kill you; you know what they did to me, and they will kill you."

"What can I do?" he said, "What do the Apaches like?"

"They like little doves."

"Then I will turn into a little dove."

He did this and she carried him home in her basket. The Apaches asked, "What is that?" and she replied, "The young of a dove; so I brought it home." But when the Apaches left the room they could hear her talking to it, and when they came in she would be still. They could not understand the words but knew she was speaking her own language, so they said, "This thing belongs to her tribe. Let us kill it."

So they went in and the chief took it in one hand and smashed it hard with the other and the pieces came through between his fingers. These pieces then flew up out of the smoke hole and turned into a flock of hawks, and they fell upon the Apaches and beat them all to death with their wings.

Then they turned back into the boy again and he and his mother started home. But when they reached the place where the grandmother had turned back they could go no farther. They turned into saguaros, one on each side of the road.

THE BIRDS AND THE FLOOD

When the waters covered all the earth two birds were hanging onto the sky with their beaks. The larger was gray with a long tail and beak; the smaller was the tiny bird that builds its nest like an olla, with only a very small opening to get in. The larger one cried and cried, but the other just held on tight and said, "Don't cry. You see that I'm littler than you, but I'm very brave. I don't give up so easily as you do. I trust in God; He will take care of those in danger if they trust in Him."

DEATH OF COYOTE

After the waters had gone down Elder Brother said to Coyote, "Don't touch that black bug, and do not eat the mesquite beans; it is dangerous to harm anything that came safe through the flood." So Coyote went on, but presently he came to the bug, and he stopped and ate it up. Then he went on to the mesquite beans and looked at them and said, "I will just taste one, and that will be all." But he stood there and ate and ate till they were all gone. And the beans swelled up in his stomach and killed him.

THE BLUEBIRD AND COYOTE

The bluebird was once a very ugly color. But there was a lake where no river flowed in or out, and the bird bathed in this four times every morning for four mornings. Every morning it sang:

> Gáto,seteúanon ima rsoñga.
> Gunañursa,
> Wuśsikâ sivany teuteunoña.
>
> (There's a blue water, it lies there.
>   I went in,
>   I am all blue.)

On the fourth morning it shed all its feathers and came out in its bare skin, but on the fifth morning it came out with blue feathers.

All this while Coyote had been watching the bird; he wanted to jump in and get it, but was afraid of the water. But on that morning he said, "How is this all your ugly color has come out of you, and now you are all blue and gay and beautiful? You are more beautiful than anything that flies in the air. I want to be blue, too." Coyote was at that time a bright green. "I only went in four times," said the bird; and it taught Coyote the song, and he went in four times, and the fifth time he came out as blue as the little bird.

That made him feel very proud, because he turned into a blue coyote. He was so proud that as he walked along he looked about on every side to see if anyone was noticing how fine and blue he was. He looked to see if his shadow was blue, too, and so he was not watching the road, and presently he ran into a stump so hard that it threw him down in the dirt and he became dust-colored all over. And to this day all coyotes are the color of dirt.

THE BOY AND THE BEAST

Once an old woman lived with her daughter, son-in-law, and grandson. They were following the trail of the Apaches. Whenever a Pima sees the track of an Apache he draws a ring around it with a stick, and then he can catch him sooner. But at night while they were asleep the Apaches came and grasped the man and woman by the hair and shook them out of their skins as one would shake corn out of a sack, and the old woman and the boy were left alone. They had to live on berries, but in one place a strange beast, big enough to swallow people, camped by the bushes. The grandmother told the boy not to go there, but he disobeyed her; he took some very sharp stones in his hands and went. As he came near the animal began to breathe and the boy just went inside of him and was swallowed all up. But with his sharp stones he cut the intestines of the beast so that he died. When the grandmother came to hunt for the boy he came out to meet her and said, "I have killed the animal."

"Oh, no; such a little boy as you are to kill such a dangerous beast!"

"But I was inside of him; just look at the stones I cut him with."

Then she went up softly and saw the holes and believed. And after that they moved down among the berries and had all they wanted to eat.

THE THIRSTY QUAILS

A quail had more than 20 children and with them she wandered over the whole country in search of water and could not find it. It was very hot and they were all crying, "Where can we get some water? Where can we get some water?" but for a long time they could find none. At last, away in the north, under a mesquite tree, they saw a pond of water, but it was very muddy and not fit to drink. But they had been wandering so many days and were so tired that they stopped in the shade, and by and by they went down one by one and drank the water, although it was so bad. But when they had all had enough it made them sick and they died.

THE NAUGHTY GRANDCHILDREN

An old woman had two bright grandchildren. She ground wheat and corn every morning to make porridge for them. One day as she put the olla on the fire outside the house, she told the children not to fight for fear they would upset the water. But they soon began quarreling, for they did not mind as well as they should, and so spilled the water, and the grandmother had to whip them. They became angry and said they were going away. She tried to make them understand why she had to whip them, but they would not listen and ran away. She ran after them, but could not catch up. She heard them whistling and followed the sound from place to place, until finally the oldest boy said, "I will turn into a saguaro, so I shall last forever, and bear fruit every summer." And the younger said, "Well, I will turn into a palo verde and stand there forever. These mountains are so bare and have nothing on them but rocks, so I will make them green." The old woman heard the cactus whistling and recognized the voice of her grandson; so she went up to it and tried to take it into her arms, and the thorns killed her.

And that is how the saguaro and palo verde came to be.

II. GROWTH

Childhood did not last long for young Indians. They were expected
to learn very quickly the duties and responsibilities of adulthood.
How were Indian children educated? Who was responsible for their
education? What role did religion play in their education? What were
the differences between the education of boys and girls? Would any
of the things taught to Indian youngsters be of value in modern industrial America? Can you tell anything about the ethics of Indian
societies from what their children were expected to do?

A Sioux Boy's Training

*Charles Eastman was a Santee Sioux, born about 1860, who grew
up in Minnesota and the Dakota Territory. He was later educated in
the East and became a doctor. These are some reminiscences of his
boyhood. (C. A. Eastman,* Indian Boyhood *(1902), 49-60.)*

It is commonly supposed that there is no systematic education of
their children among the aborigines of this country. Nothing could be
farther from the truth. All the customs of this primitive people were
held to be divinely instituted, and those in connection with the
training of children were scrupulously adhered to and transmitted
from one generation to another.

The expectant parents conjointly bent all their efforts to the task of giving the new-comer the best they could gather from a long line of ancestors. A pregnant Indian woman would often choose one of the greatest characters of her family and tribe as a model for her child. This hero was daily called to mind. She would gather from tradition all of his noted deeds and daring exploits, rehearsing them to herself when alone. In order that the impression might be more distinct, she avoided company. She isolated herself as much as possible, and wandered in solitude, not thoughtlessly, but with an eye to the impress given by grand and beautiful scenery.

The Indians believed, also, that certain kinds of animals would confer peculiar gifts upon the unborn, while others would leave so strong an adverse impression that the child might become a monstrosity. A case of hare-lip was commonly attributed to the rabbit. It was said that a rabbit had charmed the mother and given to the babe its own features. Even the meat of certain animals was denied the pregnant woman, because it was supposed to influence the disposition or features of the child.

Scarcely was the embyro warrior ushered into the world, when he was met by lullabies that speak of wonderful exploits in hunting and war. Those ideas which so fully occupied his mother's mind before his birth are now put into words by all about the child, who is as yet quite unresponsive to their appeals to his honor and ambition. He is called the future defender of his people, whose lives may depend upon his courage and skill. If the child is a girl, she is at once addressed as the future mother of a noble race.

In hunting songs, the leading animals are introduced; they come to the boy to offer their bodies for the sustenance of his tribe. The animals are regarded as his friends, and spoken of almost as tribes of people, or as his cousins, grandfathers and grandmothers. The songs of wooing, adapted as lullabies, were equally imaginative, and the suitors were often animals personified, while pretty maidens were represented by the mink and the doe.

Very early, the Indian boy assumed the task of preserving and transmitting the legends of his ancestors and his race. Almost every evening a myth, or a true story of some deed done in the past, was narrated by one of the parents or grandparents, while the boy listened with parted lips and glistening eyes. On the following evening, he was usually required to repeat it. If he was not an apt scholar, he struggled long with his task; but, as a rule, the Indian boy is a good listener and has a good memory, so that the stories were tolerably well mastered. The household became his audience, by which he was alternately criticized and applauded.

This sort of teaching at once enlightens the boy's mind and stimulates his ambition. His conception of his own future career becomes a vivid and irresistible force. Whatever there is for him to learn must be learned; whatever qualifications are necessary to a truly great man he must seek at any expense of danger and hardship. Such was the feeling of the imaginative and brave young Indian. It became apparent to him in early life that he must accustom himself to rove alone and not to fear or dislike the impression of solitude.

It seems to be a popular idea that all the characteristic skill of the Indian is instinctive and hereditary. This is a mistake. All the stoicism and patience of the Indian are acquired traits, and continual practise alone makes him master of the art of wood-craft. Physical training and dieting were not neglected. I remember that I was not allowed to have beef soup or any warm drink. The soup was for the old men. General rules for the young were never to take their food very hot, nor to drink much water.

My uncle, who educated me up to the age of fifteen years, was a strict disciplinarian and a good teacher. When I left the teepee in the morning, he would say: "Hakadah, look closely to everything you see"; and at evening, on my return, he used often to catechize me for an hour or so.

"On which side of the trees is the lighter-colored bark? On which side do they have most regular branches?"

It was his custom to let me name all the new birds that I had seen during the day. I would name them according to the color or the shape of the bill or their song or the appearance and locality of the nest—in fact, anything about the bird that impressed me as characteristic. I made many ridiculous errors, I must admit. He then usually informed me of the correct name. Occasionally I made a hit and this he would warmly commend.

He went much deeper into this science when I was a little older, that is, about the age of eight or nine years. He would say, for instance:

"How do you know that there are fish in yonder lake?"

"Because they jump out of the water for flies at mid-day."

He would smile at my prompt but superficial reply.

"What do you think of the little pebbles grouped together under the shallow water? and what made the pretty curved marks in the sandy bottom and the little sand-banks? Where do you find the fish-eating birds? Have the inlet and the outlet of a lake anything to do with the question?"

He did not expect a correct reply at once to all the voluminous questions that he put to me on these occasions, but he meant to make me observant and a good student of nature.

"Hakadah," he would say to me, "you ought to follow the example of the shunktokecha (wolf). Even when he is surprised and runs for his life, he will pause to take one more look at you before he enters his final retreat. So you must take a second look at everything you see.

"It is better to view animals unobserved. I have been a witness to their courtships and their quarrels and have learned many of their secrets in this way. I was once the unseen spectator of a thrilling battle between a pair of grizzly bears and three buffaloes—a rash act for the bears, for it was in the moon of strawberries, when the buffaloes sharpen and polish their horns for bloody contests among themselves.

"I advise you, my boy, never to approach a grizzly's den from the front, but to steal up behind and throw your blanket or a stone in front of the hole. He does not usually rush for it, but first puts his head out and listens and then comes out very indifferently and sits on his haunches on the mound in front of the hole before he makes any attack. While he is exposing himself in this fashion, aim at his heart. Always be as cool as the animal himself." Thus he armed me against the cunning of savage beasts by teaching me how to outwit them. . . .

Of this nature were the instructions of my uncle, who was widely known at that time as among the greatest hunters of his tribe.

All boys were expected to endure hardship without complaint. In savage warfare, a young man must, of course, be an athlete and used to undergoing all sorts of privations. He must be able to go without food and water for two or three days without displaying any weakness, or to run for a day and a night without any rest. He must be able to traverse a pathless and wild country without losing his way either in the day or night time. He cannot refuse to do any of these things if he aspires to be a warrior.

Sometimes my uncle would waken me very early in the morning

and challenge me to fast with him all day. I had to accept the challenge. We blackened our faces with charcoal, so that every boy in the village would know that I was fasting for the day. Then the little tempters would make my life a misery until the merciful sun hid behind the western hills.

I can scarcely recall the time when my stern teacher began to give sudden war-whoops over my head in the morning while I was sound asleep. He expected me to leap up with perfect presence of mind, always ready to grasp a weapon of some sort and to give a shrill whoop in reply. If I was sleepy or startled and hardly knew what I was about, he would ridicule me and say that I need never expect to sell my scalp dear. Often he would vary these tactics by shooting off his gun just outside of the lodge while I was yet asleep, at the same time giving blood-curdling yells. After a time I became used to this.

When Indians went upon the war-path, it was their custom to try the new warriors thoroughly before coming to an engagement. For instance, when they were near a hostile camp, they would select the novices to go after the water and make them do all sorts of things to prove their courage. In accordance with this idea, my uncle used to send me off after water when we camped after dark in a strange place. Perhaps the country was full of wild beasts, and, for aught I knew, there might be scouts from hostile bands of Indians lurking in that very neighborhood.

Yet I never objected, for that would show cowardice. I picked my way through the woods, dipped my pail in the water and hurried back, always careful to make as little noise as a cat. Being only a boy, my heart would leap at every crackling of a dry twig or distant hooting of an owl, until, at last, I reached our teepee. Then my uncle would perhaps say: "Ah, Hakadah, you are a thorough warrior," empty out the precious contents of the pail, and order me to go a second time.

Imagine how I felt! But I wished to be a brave man as much as a white boy desires to be a great lawyer or even President of the United States. Silently I would take the pail and endeavor to retrace my footsteps in the dark.

With all this, our manners and morals were not neglected. I was made to respect the adults and especially the aged. I was not allowed to join in their discussions, nor even to speak in their presence, unless requested to do so. Indian etiquette was very strict, and among the requirements was that of avoiding the direct address. A term of relationship or some title of courtesy was commonly used instead of the personal name by those who wished to show respect. We were taught generosity to the poor and reverence for the "Great Mystery." Religion was the basis of all Indian training.

I recall to the present day some of the kind warnings and reproofs that my good grandmother was wont to give me. "Be strong of heart—be patient!" she used to say. She told me of a young chief who was noted for his uncontrollable temper. While in one of his rages he attempted to kill a woman, for which he was slain by his own band and left unburied as a mark of disgrace—his body was simply covered with green grass. If I ever lost my temper, she would say:

"Hakadah, control yourself, or you will be like that young man I told you of, and lie under a *green blanket!*"

In the old days, no young man was allowed to use tobacco in any form until he had become an acknowledged warrior and had achieved a record. If a youth should seek a wife before he had reached the age of twenty-two or twenty-three, and been recognized as a brave man, he was sneered at and considered an ill-bred Indian. He must also be a skillful hunter. An Indian cannot be a good husband unless he brings home plenty of game.

These precepts were in the line of our training for the wild life.

How Fox Children Should be Brought Up

The following passage was dictated by a Fox Indian about 1900. (E. C. Parsons, ed., American Indian Life *(1922), 81-86.)*

When a boy becomes old enough to be intelligent, his parents begin to teach him how to take care of himself and act righteously. They usually tell him not to do a good many things. Children are taught not to be naughty. They are told that if they are naughty, people will have nothing to do with them. They are told that if they are naughty, people will talk about them. And children are told not to steal anything from their neighbors. Moreover, children are taught not to talk to people. If they see any one going by their place, they should hold their tongues, nor should they laugh.

And they also tell children not to visit other people too often. "Every time they see you going anywhere they would say that you are looking for something good to eat, if you go visiting too often," is what children are told. So children do not often visit too much.

They likewise tell children not to gamble. They tell them that they might be lucky and win, but that it would not benefit them. And they tell them that it is just as bad to lose. They caution them in this way: "If you win, people will see your winnings and will try to get you to gamble. And if you do, you will surely lose all that you have won. And yet it is not right to be over-quiet. If you are quiet and well off, that is not quite right either. If you have a lot of horses, people will be jealous of you. Some one might want some of your property, and you would not give it to him. That is how it will be.

"The best way is to be kindly to every one, to speak kind words, to treat your friends nicely, to keep your heart clean, and not to talk meanly. If you do this, you will have a number of friends. And when you are a young boy, do not fight with other boys. If any one speaks badly to you, do not answer him. Let it go. This is one of the best things you can do. And if you see some one doing something, you must hold your peace; do not be the one to start the news. Do not tell what you saw him or her do. If you spread the report they will hate you. They will become your enemies."

And there is another thing which boys are told. Boys are told not to tattle to any one. They are told not to be too intimate with girls. It is not a right thing for a boy to do. They are warned: "If you do that, people will be jealous of you."

And there is another thing they are warned. "When there are many people, when something is going on, don't go over there, and try to show off. That will not benefit you. You may go to the crowd and see what is going on, but behave yourself. And if any one asks you a question, you are to tell the person that you know nothing about it. That is the best way to keep out of trouble."

And there is another thing which young men are told, which is: "If some one asks you to do a favor, you must always do it for him. Some time in the near future they will come around again and ask another favor of you. If you refuse, you straightway will begin to have trouble. But you should always do a favor for any one, so as to please them."

And another thing, young men are told, not to fear ashes: "By fasting and painting your face with ashes, you may get a blessing from the Manitou. If you do the right thing, you will surely be blessed. If you are afraid, the Manitou will know it. People claim that fasting and blackening one's face with ashes is one of the best things that they can do. In the early days it was said that if one fasted long to obtain a blessing from the Manitou, he often went on the war-path successfully; or he killed people by fasting so long. Such was the blessing the person obtained. And you can go and kill game easily. You may become a leader in anything. If there is a war you may become a leader. And you will always bring your men back safe and sound. They will not be killed by the enemy. You will surely be blessed by the Manitou if you take an interest in fasting, and are not afraid of doing so. After you have fasted long enough, if you desire anything, you will obtain it. So fasting is the right thing to do. And if you do this, you must get up early—before our grandfather, the Sun, rises. If anything happens to people where you are, after a few years, nothing will happen to you: you will not be destroyed. This is the only way you can live again. All the people will be benefited by you. This is the best life there is." And this is why children are taught to fast.

Boys are told that if they see an animal they must not destroy it. For if they destroy animals, they themselves will not live very long. Boys are also taught to be good hunters.

Boys are taught nearly everything so that they can get along nicely with their wives after they are married. They are told that if they are hustlers many girls will wish to marry them.

Of course this is after they have grown to be young men. Up to that time they are merely made to fast. And by fasting, is how they reach old age. Also children are made to fast when any one dies. And they also tell children not to make a noise when some one dies; and not to play where the body is. And they tell boys not to refuse if they are asked to do something. "If you do what people who have lost their relatives ask you, they will be well satisfied with you. And some day you will exchange positions. If you ask them a favor at that time, they will willingly do it," is what boys are told.

And this is what boys are told when they are growing up: "If you are asked to be a ceremonial attendant at clan festivals, you must do it. By doing them the favor of waiting on them, you will benefit your own life. And any time you are asked to do anything you must always do it, so as to please the people.''

And after they grow up, they are told not to bother too much with girls, especially if they have sisters of their own. They are told, ''Sometime you may be desired as a son-in-law. But if you bother with many girls, while going with one, they will think you are a nobody.'' And they tell boys not to be intimate with girls unless they plan to marry them. They are told, ''You must not say anything evil to women: if you do, you will be talking evilly to your own sisters.

''And if you are going with a girl, if you are engaged to her, you must marry her, and treat her rightly. You must go home with her and stay with your father-in-law and your mother-in-law. You must treat them as nicely as you can. And you should hunt for your mother-in-law and your father-in-law. If you treat your wife meanly, every one will talk about you. And that will make it bad for you. At all gatherings people will talk about you, saying how badly you treat your wife. The people will say many things about you, though you may not know it. They will say you are jealous. And in that way people will always refuse you favors. You will be treating your wife badly, if you pay no attention to the old people.

''You must obey your parents. It is the right thing to obey one's parents. And boys who do not obey their parents are the worst boys to-day.

''If you know any one has something of his own, you must not ask him for it, nor must you steal it. It is not right to steal. If you steal or ask for the thing you want, all the people will be afraid of you. You are nothing but a beggar. Every one will say that to you. They will call you a beggar.''

Now when boys are beginning to be grown up, they are told: ''You must not turn against your friends; you must be kind-hearted. And you must not bother with any woman or girl who is married to another man. You should not try to 'cut him out.' It is dangerous to do that.'' This is one of the most important things they try to get boys to understand. By doing what is forbidden they might get into trouble; and they might end their lives. Many boys end their lives before they are middle-aged by not listening to their parents.

And girls are taught a little differently from boys. Of course they tell girls, in the beginning, the same thing, that is, how to take care of themselves. They teach girls that if they obey the rules they will have an easier life as they grow older. After they are old enough they teach them how to do things. And they also make them fast. They are asked to fast so that adversity shall not strike them when they grow up. They make girls fast for four days. They make them fast all winter, especially when they are beginning to be young ladies. The reason why they make them fast is that they are supposed to dream of something that will take them through their life. That is why they do not take regular meals like others, to prepare for a long life.

And they teach them to do something for themselves, especially when they grow up. They teach them work, suitable for women. They teach them to learn to make mattings and how to make sacks. They also teach them how to make moccasins and beadwork. Girls are told that they can get along nicely if they learn these things before they are married. They are told, "You will be benefited by doing this for your husband. Your relatives will be benefited by you."

And girls are told: "If you are a moral girl, your father-in-law and mother-in-law will treat you as nicely as they can. And they will love you. If you are quiet and well-behaved, you will be much better off than those girls who do not mind. Men do not care for girls who do not mind and who are immoral. If you do not mind and are immoral, no man will have you for his wife." That is why girls are taught to be good.

After they learn to make things, they are taught to cook meals. Girls are told that by doing so, they are leading themselves the right way. "By so doing you are leading yourself an easy way. Sometime you may grow up and make your own home." That is why girls are told to be willing workers.

And girls are told not to go off and live with other people. Of course people would like a girl to live with them a few days. But a few days later they might turn her out, especially if she were lazy. People do not wish to support a lazy person. This is why girls are taught to cook.

And after they are married, girls are especially told not to say anything about other persons, and not to feel unfriendly towards them. And they are told not to have any quarrels with other people, for that is not a right thing to do. They are told to be kind towards the people and not to have quarrels with any one. "This is the best way, to be friendly with every one. By so doing, the people will feel kindly towards you. They will always say a good word for you. People do not think anything of a mean person. If you are mean, some day some one will turn against you. Some persons are dangerous. They have secret ways to kill people.'' This is why girls are told not to be mean, or say mean things to other persons. And some girls hate their parents for telling them this. But it is a rule that children should be taught. The reason parents tell girls this, is because they love them so well. They are teaching them so they can attain an old age. Girls who were not taught, do anything they please. They do not care what they do. They spoil themselves.

Girls are supposed to be taught till they are married. After a girl is married, she has full control of herself, and may do whatever she thinks best. But it is best to follow the rules forever, to be kind to one's husband and the people. It is pretty hard to lead a righteous life.

When girls begin to have children they are told to be kind to their children and love them, and not to do anything bad to them. And they are taught that if they live quietly to an old age, they themselves will be the only relations they have.

And before children are well grown, they dare not go any place by themselves. Of course boys are different: they can go any place they please. And girls dare not do so, unless they have a good reason for it. They are taught to always be at home and do the work. They are told: ''If you grow to be a young lady, if you walk around and do not do any work, people will not think anything of you. They will always talk about you. They will say that all you are good for, is to walk from place to place. They will say you are looking for a place to get your meals. They will say that you are looking for a place where you can get the finest food. They will say many things about you. They will even say that you are worse than a man. Every time you are on the road they will say, 'There goes a woman who goes about looking for good meals for herself.' '' That is the reason why they desire a girl to be able to do things so that she can support herself after she is grown. That is why they tell girls to obey their parents. Their parents have had good experience and know what they are talking about.

And when girls arrive at puberty, they are told not to marry a divorced man. They are told to marry a young man. In the early days, people used to say to each other when girls married divorced men: ''It is not natural for a girl to marry a divorced man, nor for a young man to marry a divorced woman.'' They told girls that if they married young men, that they would be benefited by getting horses, and so on. And a girl is told to look around and get the right kind of a boy. In the early days, they liked boys who killed game, trapped, sold furs, and so got money; but nowadays they tell girls to look around for boys that have horses, homes, everything they want. They say, "That's the right kind of a young man to marry—one that can support you."

Girls are also told: "When you are staying with your father-in-law and with your mother-in-law, you are supposed to help them in their work. When your mother-in-law begins doing anything, you must ask her if you may do it." A girl is taught this so that she can get along nicely after she is married. Girls are told: "If you don't do these things, people will talk about you, and say how lazy you are. And people will not like you." This is the reason why a girl is taught all manner of work.

And all girls are taught the same things. And in this way, they lead themselves the right way.

A Fox Indian Girlhood

This passage contains more of the autobiography of the Fox woman who told about having a baby in Chapter I. Compare what she remembers about her childhood with what the previous selection said Fox children should be taught. (Michelson, "Autiobiography of a Fox Woman," 297-309.)

Well, I shall now tell what happened to me. From the time when I was six years old is perhaps when I begin to recollect it. Of course (I do) not (recollect it) fully; I forget once in a great while (some days) each year back.

Well, I played with dolls when I made them. (And) when I played with them I would make one large doll. Now they would be supposed to be many children. And that large doll, I would pretend, would do the cooking. Of course I would do the cooking in my play. And many of us would eat together when we ate, I pretended. And then I made little wickiups for the dolls to live in.

When I was perhaps seven years old I began to practice sewing for my dolls. But I sewed poorly. I used to cry because I did not know how to sew. Nor could I persuade my mother to (do it) when I said to her, "Make it for me." "You will know how to sew later on; that is why I shall not make them for you. That is how one learns to sew, by practicing sewing for one's dolls. That is why one has dolls, namely, to make everything for them—their clothing and moccasins." And so I would always practice sewing for my dolls.

When I was perhaps eight years old I began to like to swim. If we were living near where a river flowed by, we girls always would swim. There were many of us. Although we were scolded, yet when we could do so secretly we would go swimming. Some would be whipped because they did not mind. As for me, I was never whipped as I was the only girl (my parents) had. I would only be severely scolded when I did not mind when I was forbidden (anything). And I was made to fast when I did not pay attention. And I was forbidden to go with the other little girls, that is, the very naughty ones. "They might get you (into their habits), as they will not know how to make anything when they grow up in the future if they do not try to make anything. That is the way you will be if you do not try to make any-thing, if you merely loaf around," I would be told when I was made to fast. I was fed at noon. But soon, within several days, I had forgot-ten what I was forbidden. Again I was told, "Do not sleep anywhere (in the wickiups) of the little girls with whom you play. Come back to where we live while it is still daylight. Do not be out some place in the night. Play with them now and then."

Well, when I was nine years old I was able to help my mother. It was in spring when planting was begun that I was told. "Plant some-thing to be your own." Sure enough I did some planting. When they began to hoe weeds where it was planted, I was told "Say! You weed in your field." My hoe was a little hoe. And soon the hoeing would cease. I was glad.

When (we) ceased bothering where it was planted, I was unwilling to do anything. But when I would be told, "When you finish this, then you may go and play with the little girls," I was willing. I then surely played violently with the children. We played tag as we en-joyed it.

And at the time when what we planted was mature, I was told,

"Say! You must try to cook what you have raised." Surely then I tried to cook. After I cooked it, my parents tasted it. "What she has raised tastes very well," they said to me. "And she has cooked it very carefully," I would be told. I was proud when they said that to me. As a matter of fact I was just told so that I might be encouraged to cook. And I thought, "It's probably true."

And when I was ten years old I ceased caring for dolls. But I still liked to swim. But when I said to my mother, "May I go swimming?" she said to me, "Yes. You may wash your grandmother's waist for her, and you may wash mine also," I was told. I was made to wash (anything) little. Surely I would not feel like asking, "May I go swimming," as I was afraid of the washing. Now as a matter of fact the reason why I was treated so was to encourage me to learn how to wash.

"That is why I treat you like that, so that you will learn how to wash," my mother told me. "No one continues to be taken care of forever. The time soon comes when we lose sight of the one who takes care of us. I never got to know how my mother looked. My father's sister brought me up. To-day I treat you just as she treated me. She did not permit me to be just fooling around. Why, even when I was eight years old I knew how to cook very well. When my father's sister was busy with something, I did the cooking," she said to me. I did not believe her when she said that, for I was then ten years old and was just beginning to cook well, and I knew how to sew but I was poor at it. At that time when my mother woke up, she said to me, "Wake up, you may fetch some water. And go get some little dry sticks so we may start the fire," she said to me. When I was unwilling I was nevertheless compelled. That is the way I was always treated.

Soon, moreover, I was told, "This is your little ax," when a little ax was brought. I was glad. "This is your wood-strap," I was told. My mother and I would go out to cut wood; and I carried the little wood that I had cut on my back. She would strap them for me. She instructed me how to tie them up. Soon I began to go a little ways off by myself to cut wood.

And when I was eleven years old I likewise continually watched her as she would make bags. "Well, you try to make one," she said to me. She braided up one little bag for me. She instructed me how to make it. Sure enough, I nearly learned how to make it, but I made it very badly. I was again told, "You make another." It was somewhat larger. And soon I knew how to make it very well. Then surely I was unwilling to make them. At first I was willing to make them as I did not know how to make them very well. But I was constrained to keep on making them. During the winters I kept on making them. Moreover, at that time a little rush mat was woven for me. "Make this," I was told. I tried to make it. Later on I finished it. I made it extremely poorly. Soon I began to help my mother after I knew how to make rush mats.

She would be very proud after I had learned to make anything. "There, you will make things for yourself after you take care of yourself. That is why I constrain you to make anything, not to treat you meanly. I let you do things so that you may make something. If you happen to know how to make everything when you no longer see me, you will not have a hard time in any way. You will make your own possessions. My father's sister, the one who took care of me, treated me so. That is why I know how to make any little thing. 'She is in the habit of treating me meanly,' I thought, when she ordered me to make something all the time. Now as a matter of fact she treated me well. When I knew about it, I would think, 'why she must have treated me very well.' And that is why I treat you so to-day. So very likely when you think of me, you think, 'she treats me meanly.' It is because I am fond of you and wish you to know how to make things. If I were not fond of you, I would not order you around (to do things). (If I were not fond of you) I would think, 'I don't care what she does.' If you are intelligent when you are grown and recollect how I treated you, you will think, 'I declare! My mother treated me well.' Or if you are bad you will not remember me when I am gone. And this. Though you know how to make things you will not make anything. That is what you will do if you are bad. I do not wish you to be that way. I desire that you take care of yourself quietly," my mother told me.

And again, when I was twelve years old, I was told, "Come, try to make these." (They were) my own moccasins. "You may start to make them for yourself after you know how to make them. For you already know how to make them for your dolls. That is the way you are to make them," I was told. She only cut them out for me. And when I made a mistake she ripped it out for me. "This is the way you are to make it," I was told. Finally I really knew how to make them.

And then a small belt of yarn was put on the sticks for me. A little was started for me. "Try to make this one," I was told. I began to try to make it. Later on I surely knew how to make it. Then I kept on making belts of yarn. My mother was pleased when I learned how to make anything.

At that time I knew how to cook well. When my mother went any place, she said to me. "You may cook the meal." Moreover, when she made mats I cooked the meals. "You may get accustomed to cooking, for it is almost time for you to live outside. You will cook for yourself when you live outside," I would be told.

Soon I was told, "Well, begin to try to weave; you may wish to make these mats." Then I began to try to weave. Later I knew how to weave very well. Then I began to help my mother all the time. She was proud when I continued to learn how to make anything.

And then I was thirteen years old. "Now is the time when you must watch yourself; at last you are nearly a young woman. Do not forget this which I tell you. You might ruin your brothers if you are not careful. The state of being a young woman is evil. The manitous hate it. If any one is blessed by a manitou, if he eats with a young woman he is then hated by the one who blessed him and the (manitou) ceases to think of him. That is why it is told us, 'be careful' and why we are told about it beforehand. At the time when you are a young woman, whenever you become a young woman, you are to hide yourself. Do not come into your wickiup. That is what you are to do." She frightened me when she told me.

Lo, sure enough when I was thirteen and a half years old, I was told, "Go get some wood and carry it on your back." It was nearly noon when I started out. When I was walking along somewhere, I noticed something strange about myself. I was terribly frightened at being in that condition. I did not know how I became that way. "This must be the thing about which I was cautioned when I was told," I thought.

I went and laid down in the middle of the thick forest there. I was crying, as I was frightened. It was almost the middle of summer after we had done our hoeing. After a while my mother got tired of waiting for me. She came to seek me. Soon she found me. I was then crying hard.

"Come, stop crying. It's just the way with us women. We have been made to be that way. Nothing will happen to you. You will have gotten over this now in the warm weather. Had it happened to you in winter you would have had a hard time. You would be cold when you bathed as you would have to jump into the water four times. That is the way it is when we first have it. Now, to-day, as it is warm weather, you may swim as slowly as you like when you swim," I was told. "Lie covered up. Do not try to look around. I shall go and make (a wickiup) for you," I was told.

I was suffering very much there in the midst of the brush. And it was very hot.

It was in the evening when I was told, "At last I have come for you. I have built (a place) for you to live in. Cover your face. Do not think of looking any place." I was brought there to the small wickiup. And I was shut off by twigs all around. There was brush piled up so that I could not see through it. There was only a little space where I lived to cook outside. My grandmother must have made it a size so that there was only room for us to lie down in.

"I shall fetch your grandmother to be here with you," my mother told me. It was another old woman. As a matter of fact the reason she was brought there was for to give me instructions. I did not eat all day long. The next day I was told, "We shall fetch things for you to use in cooking." I was not hungry as I was frightened. The next day my grandmother went to eat. It was only as long as she (took) when she went to eat that I was alone, but I was afraid. In the evening I was brought little buckets to cook with, any little thing to eat, water and wood. Then for the first time I cooked.

And my grandmother would keep on giving me instructions there, telling me how to lead a good life. She really was a very old woman. Surely she must have spoken the truth in what she had been saying to me. "My grandchild," she would say to me, "soon I shall tell you how to live an upright life. To-day you see how old I am. I did exactly what I was told. I tried and thought how to live an upright life. Surely I have reached an old age," she told me. "That is the way you should do, if you listen to me as I instruct you. Now as for your mother, I began giving her instructions before she was grown up, every time I saw her. Because she was my relative is why I gave her instructions, although she was well treated by her father's sister by whom she was reared. That is why she knows how to make things which belong to the work of us women. If you observe the way your mother makes anything, you would do well, my grandchild. And this. As many of us as entered young womanhood, fasted. It was very many days: some fasted ten days; some four, five, every kind of way. To-day, to be sure, things are changing. When I was a young woman I fasted eight days. We always fasted until we were grown up,'' my grandmother told me.

My mother only came to fetch me water and little sticks of wood so that I might kindle a fire when I cooked. And we made strings. That is what we did.

"Do not touch your hair: it might all come off. And do not eat sweet things. And if what tastes sour is eaten, one's teeth will come out. It is owing to that saying that we are afraid to eat sweet things,'' my grandmother told me. She always gave me good advice from time to time. ''Well, there is another thing. Now the men will think you are mature as you have become a young woman, and they will be desirous of courting you. If you do not go around bashfully, for a long time they will not have the audacity to court you. When there is a dance, when there are many boys saying all sorts of funny things, if you do not notice it, they will be afraid of you for a very long time. If you laugh over their words, they will consider you as naught. They will begin bothering you right away. If you are immoral your brothers will be ashamed, and your mother's brothers. If you live quietly they will be proud. They will love you. If you are only always making something in the same place where you live, they will always give you something whenever they get it. And your brothers will believe you when you say anything to them. When one lives quietly the men folks love one. And there is another thing. Some of the girls of our generation are immoral. If one goes around all the time with those who are immoral, they would get one in the habit of being so, as long as one has not much intelligence. Do not go around with the immoral ones, my grandchild,'' my grandmother told me. ''And this. You are to treat any aged person well. He (she) is thought of by the manitou: because he (she) has conducted his (her) life carefully is why he (she) reached an old age. Do not talk about anyone. Do not lie. Do not steal. If you practice stealing, you will be wretched. Do not (be stingy) with a possession of which you are fond. (If you are stingy) you will not get anything. If you are generous you will (always) get something. Moreover, do not go around and speak crossly toward anyone. You must be equally kind to (every) old person. That, my grandchild, is a good way to do.'' my grandmother said to me. She was indeed always instructing me what to do.

Soon I had lived there ten days. ''Well, at last you may go and take a bath.'' my mother said to me. We started to the river. ''Take off your waist.'' I was told. After I had taken it off I leaped into the water. Then, ''I am going to peck you with something sharp.'' I was told. I was pecked all over. ''And now on your lower part.'' I was told. ''Only use your skirt as a breechcloth,'' is what I was told. I was also pecked on my thighs. ''It will be that you will not menstruate much if the blood flows plentifully.'' I was told. I was made to suffer very much. I put on other garments. I threw away those which I had formerly been wearing around. And then for the first time I looked around to see. And again I had to cook alone for myself outside for ten days. After ten days I again went to bathe. And then for the first time I began to eat indoors with (the others).

I told my mother. ''My grandmother has always been instructing me what I should do,'' I said to her. She laughed. ''That is why I went after her, so she would instruct you thoroughly in what is right. 'She might listen to her,' is what I thought of you.''

And I began to be told to make something more than ever. Moreover, when she made a basket, she said to me, ''You (make one).'' I would make a tiny basket. Later on the ones which I made were large ones. And then I was fifteen years old.

''You may now try to sew bead and appliqué ribbon work. If you know how to sew you are to make things to wear when you dance. If it is known that you can already sew, (people) will hire you. Not merely that. You will be paid. You will be benefited by knowing how to sew,'' my mother told me. Then indeed I began to practice sewing. It took me a long time to sew well. It (must have) taken me two years to sew well. From then I was always making something.

I was sixteen years old when we were making mats in the summer. In the winter we were making sacks and yarn belts, (and) we were sewing appliqué ribbon work and bead work. Behold, it was true that I was constantly asked (to make) something, (and) I would be paid. ''That is why,'' I would be told, ''I continuously told you to learn to know how to make things. After these mats are completed, and any one is given them, soon he (she) (will) give something in return. And also in regard to these sacks, when (anyone) is given them, he (she) gives something in return, no doubt. That is why one is willing to make things, because they are benefited by what is made,'' I was told. Lo, surely when I began to realize it, what I had been told was true.

III. LOVE AND MARRIAGE

Indian young people usually married at the first opportunity; the men as soon as they were competent enough hunters to provide for a family, and the women soon after reaching childbearing age. How did the Indians court their lovers? How free were men or women to marry whom they wished? Was divorce common? Why? Who initiated it? Were the Indians sexually moral? Why? How prepared for marriage and the problems of living together did the Indians seem to be?

A Cree Couple

The Cree Indians inhabited the region surrounding the northern shores of the upper Great Lakes. The following excerpt is from a life history told to anthropologist Ruth Landes. (R. Landes, The Ojibwa Woman *(1938), 233-39.)*

Tupuhsi and her husband Buhnah were members of a Cree group living intimately with the Ojibwa, and sharing their customs. For about five years Tupuhsi and her husband lived happily. "He was a good hunter and made a good living. They had only one child, a boy. When he was about four or five years old, the boy sickened, and after a long time he died. They had done everything to cure him, she had even tried her Power, but nothing helped. She used to wonder where

Buhnah went sometimes. He used to stay out late. And then when the boy died, she was sad. She missed her little boy . . . she was so lonely. . . . but the worst of all was that her husband would go out in the night, stay out all night, and only come home in the morning. He never spoke to his wife, but he would just come in and lie down to sleep. She never asked him where he went, she simply continued working, and pretended to pay no attention to him. But she wondered and wondered where he went at night. Each night he went out, and each day he slept, and always towards evening he woke up and ate. He would never say a word to anyone. One time he took his sack and took out an otter skin and cut it into strips. He took a comb and combed his hair, and braided it in two long braids. He took the strips of otter skin and wound them around the braids. He put on his nice clothes, and nice moccasins, but he did not put any paint on his face. Then he took a new blanket, and went out again. His wife made up her mind to follow him. She followed him among the wigwams to the very end of the village. Her husband went into the very last wigwam. She peeped in and saw two old people and a young girl. The old people had already gone to bed. Just the woman was sitting up, and Buhnah sat down right beside her. Right away she started caressing his braids. Tupuhsi stood there for a long time and watched them. Then she went home and went to sleep.

"The next morning her husband returned home and slept all day. She did not say anything. But she cried an awful lot, and her mother-in-law spoke to her while she was crying. She told her to stop crying, that nothing or no one would have pity on her anyway, and people were beginning to take notice of her husband's being dressed up all the time; they were beginning to think of the pair as no good on account of Buhnah's carrying on. Yet he continued. She made up her mind to do something. After Buhnah went out again that night, she went to bed and pretended to be asleep. Then she got up very quietly, washed her face, combed her hair, and braided her hair into two long braids at the back, tying on bunches of ribbon. She put on new moccasins, and a good dress and waist. Then she took a shawl and wrapped it around her. She took the leather strap she used for carrying wood, and then she went out very quietly. She went to her little son's grave, and cried very hard. Then she went along and came to some grey willow trees, and she tied her leather strap to the trees and said, 'What is there left for me to live for? No one cares for me, and my boy is gone. So I too will go and join my boy.' Then she put the leather around her neck. But before she was ready to do this (i.e., hang herself), someone grabbed her by the shoulders and said, 'No, you cannot do this to yourself because you are too good and nice-looking. I know what's been on your mind since you learned about your husband, but don't worry yourself about him. I will take you away from here so that you will not know what he is doing. I will take you where your parents are, and you will never leave them again as long as you live. (Troubled wives often return to the parental lodge for security, and even to insure actual protection against a difficult husband, who may pursue them. The parental lodge is the one relatively safe base in the world; so the son-in-law who lives with his wife's people is on enemy territory, living there by a courteous waiver, and must conduct himself with suitable prudence.) I have been watching you for a long time, and so I know what's been on your mind.' He took her by the hand and led her away from there. He said, 'Get ready right away if you want to take anything along with you. And please hurry up.' She never said one word while he was talking. She did not know what to do, but anyway she went along with him, and he took her to her wigwam. 'I will come here with my canoe. Be sure and hurry.' So he went and after he was gone she stood there puzzled. . . . who was he? She could not recognize his voice either. Then she went to the wigwam of Buhnah's second wife. She peeped in again and saw her husband sleeping with the woman, and she got very mad. She was wondering what to do when this same man came up to her again, put his hands on her shoulders, and said, 'Come away from there, and go with me. It will not do you any good to stand there and look at him. He's not good enough for you. But I will try and be good and make up to you for all the misery you've been through.' So she returned with him to her own wigwam. He told her to take the things she liked best, and to hurry. She went into her wigwam and took some things. She had a little pup and she took him along too. Then the man took her down to the canoe, and they went away. She did not paddle but just sat in the canoe (a sweetheart, wife, or daughter paddles for a man, but not a stranger).

"They went through a big portage, and after they got on the other side, the man stopped and made a fire (this is ordinarily the job of sweetheart, wife, or daughter) and made some tea. It was still night. She tried to see his face, but he had his head down, and she could not tell yet who he was. He gave her some good things to eat. He began to play with the little pup. She thought to herself, 'Whoever he is, he must be very silly.' The man said to her without looking at her, 'I know what you are thinking of me. You think I'm silly because I am playing with your pup.'' Then she began to fear him (because he manifested the supernatural power of telepathy). After their lunch, they went down again, and started out with the canoe. He said, 'There are rapids near here. We will not go over them until morning.' So they stopped close by. He told her she could sleep in the canoe, and he got out and lay down in the grass (this continence of the man is the ultimate expression of respect), and they slept.''

For several days he scrupulously avoided Tupuhsi, although they were alone on deserted islands. After the passage of a few days they became more friendly, though still shy. ''He asked her if they could not stay there for a couple of days and dry the moose he had killed (this is a wife's work). She said it was all right. Then they made a little wigwam. He told her that he had cared for her all the time she had lived with Buhnah. He had heard people say that she was blamed for the death of her little son, therefore her husband did not want her any more; and he had found out that Buhnah was flirting with another woman. Then he made up his mind to look after her, and he started spying on her. He loved her all that time, and that was why he never married anyone else. He never bothered her while she was married to Buhnah, but when he knew what Buhnah was doing, he realized that he had not waited in vain for her. And he told her that he wanted to marry her no matter what she had done. Tupuhsi only now understood why her husband did not care for her; but it was not true that she had caused her son's death, for she had tried her best to save him.

''So they slept there that night. They stayed there for three or four days drying meat. Once they saw two men coming in a canoe, and she ran and hid. She did not want them to see her. The men came right up to the wigwam and said, 'Oh, this is where you are making meat.' He said, 'Yes,' and they said again, 'We have been sent here by the people back there to look for you. Your grandmother is worried about you because she thinks you are lost, and also one woman is lost.' He said, 'We are not lost. We know where we are. And also we know what we are doing.' Then he gave them some meat (to buy their good-will) and they went away. Tupuhsi returned to the wigwam, and he told her what the men had said. She was very frightened, but he said, 'Please don't be like that, scared. . . . I will take care of you so that no harm will come to you. Don't you know that I love you an awful lot? and it hurts me to know that you don't trust me and are afraid.' He took her in his arms then. Right there she said she would care for him. So he told her to get ready, that they would go to her parents (an announcement of marriage).

"So they went, and her mother saw them coming. She went in and told her old man, 'Our daughter is coming, but with another man.' And her father said, 'I suppose she is doing something to make us ashamed.' The old woman went down and met her daughter, and kissed her. She also cried for her little grandson. But the old man did not come out at all; he was worried, and ashamed of his daughter. She told her mother everything that Buhnah had done to her, and how she had been blamed for the death of her little boy. Her mother went in to see the old man and told him all about it, but he did not say anything. The man (second husband) made a wigwam close by, and this is where they lived. Tupuhsi had a young brother, and he was very proud of his new brother-in-law because he knew he was good to his sister. She never lacked anything. Her new husband was very good to her, and also he was a good hunter. The old man got over his shame soon for he saw that he had a far better son-in-law this time.

"All the Indians came together for a celebration before ricemaking time. Buhnah came too with his wife. The men played the moccasin game, and the women played squaw hockey and other kinds of Indian games, and danced. Tupuhsi's husband told her to join in the women's games. One time she was asked to play squaw hockey because she had nice clothes and wore nice shoes, and people wished for her clothes (in the gambling stakes). So she played. This other woman was playing too—the one who took Buhnah away from her. She was poorly dressed and her old moccasins were no good. As they were playing, she was in Tupuhsi's way. Tupuhsi pushed her over and as she fell, her feet went up. And Tupuhski said laughing (in insulting ridicule), 'Look at her old moccasins! They look like lynx paws!' Tupuhsi's side won the game. After she went home, her husband said, 'Don't do that to tease anyone, especially that woman.' So she never said anything again because she always did what her husband told her.

"Then the next day, the man played the moccasin game. Her husband went, and took a gun and blanket, and his brother-in-law went with him. Buhnah was to play against him; he also brought a gun. Before they started to play Buhnah was working on his gun, and the shell fell out. This young man (the second husband) took the shell, and Buhnah did not know that it had fallen out. While they were playing, Buhnah knew that his side was getting beat. He took his gun again and started to play with it. Of course the young man was watching him, and he knew what was going to happen. Sure enough, Buhnah pulled the trigger when the gun was pointed towards him (in the course of the game). Buhnah started to shout (the murderous war-whoop), but there was nothing but gun powder in the gun. The man that was supposed to be shot laughed and said, 'Here man, here is your shell. You forgot to put it back in', and he said also, 'I have a knife in my pocket.' He drew his knife out, but as he was going to stab Buhnah, his brother-in-law grabbed his hand and took the knife away from him, and took him home. Buhnah went home also, and soon they saw him paddling away with his wife. All the men yelled after him, saying he was a coward. Tupuhsi's husband told her that they would stay there only four days more. So after four days, they went to a different place to make rice, and Buhnah happened to be there also. Tupuhsi's husband told her not to go back in the bush to cut wigwam poles, that his brother-in-law and he would cut them, for he knew that Buhnah intended to kill her with the axe she would use. Sure enough, Buhnah shouted that the women should cut the wigwam poles. Tupuhsi did not go, as her husband had told her not to, so Buhnah failed to kill her. Again he moved away.

"After ricemaking time they moved back to their own place. The railroad was under construction now, and her husband worked on it. The white men thought a lot of him because he was a good worker. One summer, about three years later, she was washing at a kind of dock. Her brother, now a grown man, was inside the wigwam with a sore foot. While she was washing, someone spoke to her, 'You make me mad when you are so happily married, and also because you did not care that our boy died, and the man you are married to now is very proud.' She answered, "You did not care either when our boy died. You were the first to marry.' Then he pushed her into the water. She could not swim, and each time she came to the surface and grabbed the dock, he stepped on her hand and kicked it off. Each time she yelled. Her brother heard her, and he came out, though he could hardly walk. He saw this man standing there. He had a stick and came up behind Buhnah, hit him with the stick, and knocked him into the water. Then his sister had time to get out of the water, and they both went away from there. Buhnah came ashore too, and he ran away as fast as he could. Her husband came home from work as she was putting on dry clothes, and her brother told him all about it, how he saved his sister from getting drowned. Her husband was very mad, but he did not follow Buhnah.

"The following summer, while they were again living there, Buhnah came there with two men in a canoe. He told Tupuhsi's husband that he had come for her, that she was his wife, and that he was going to take her away whether or not he (the husband) would let her go. And the husband said, 'No, you will not take her, away from me as long as I'm alive. You cast her aside for another woman, and I saved her when she was going to take her life on account of you, and I care for her an awful lot, and I'm going to fight to hold her.' Buhnah went right up to him and started to fight. Buhnah was thrown down and he cried. 'All right, men, come and help me!' But the men did not move. The two men kept right on fighting, and Buhnah was getting beaten very badly because he was older. He said he was going to take Tupuhsi anyway, and her husband said, 'No, Buhnah, you're not going to take her away because I'm going to kill you, because you are always bothering us. We never bother you, and you've done enough to us now, and I cannot stand any more from you. Twice you nearly killed my wife. You did not care for her. You're just jealous because I'm proud of her. So I'm going to kill you now with my own hands so you will never both us any more.' He started to hit Buhnah harder, and one of his blows knocked him dead. The men just stood there, looking on. After he knew he was dead, he told the man to take the body home, and they did. Some people tried to get him into trouble by telling the white men, but they couldn't because the white men believed his story, and they also liked him. So he was free. . . . nobody ever bothered them any more.". . . .

Marriages of a Fox Woman

This selection continues the life story of the Fox woman of whom you have read in the preceeding chapters. (Michelson, "Autobiography of a Fox Woman," 309-15, 321-27.)

Now when I was more than seventeen, while living outside somewhere, after two days, late at night while I was still sleeping (some one) said to me, "Wake up." (The person) was holding a match, and lit it. Lo, it was a man when I looked at him. I was as frightened as possible. I trembled as I was frightened. When I ordered him away, (my voice) did not (sound) natural when I spoke. I was barely able to speak to him. And from then on, now and then men tried to come to me. I always had been instructed what was proper. When it was known (what kind of a person) I (was), they began to try to court me.

Then I was instructed, "Well, when you are twenty, then you may desire to take a husband. Whoever is the one whom you are going to take as your husband, he alone is the one with whom you are to talk when you begin to talk with (a man). Do not talk to many. It is not right for women to have many friends. Their husband(s) will not treat them well as they are jealous when they know what (their wives) have been doing. That indeed is why (women) are forbidden to have many friends." That is what I was told.

Then soon when I was eighteen, in the spring at the time when (people) begin to pick strawberries. I accompanied a young woman when we were strawberrying. "We will see one," she would say to me. Then she would say to me. "I am just joshing you." As a matter of fact she and one young man had made arrangements to see each other over there.

Soon he came over there. They were well acquainted with each other and treated each other kindly. She was helped by him when she was picking strawberries. She kept coming to me to get me to go with her some place. Soon he came with another young man. Then this young woman got me to talk to his fellow young man. "He will not do anything: you may talk together quietly," that woman told me. As often as we went anywhere those men came. Finally I surely began to talk to that young man. And then we four went around (together) a great deal. It surely was enjoyable (to hear them) say funny things. Then it

was that I always wished to see him right away when I went anywhere, that is after I had seen him.

Of course many men tried to get me to talk with them. Soon it was
known (what kind of a person I was). My, but they scolded me
severely. Another young man had been selected for me to take as
husband. (The other one) and I were already well acquainted.

"You had better take a husband right away," I was told. " 'When
you are twenty, you shall take a husband.' I told you formerly when I
was instructing you. And I forbade you to go around with immoral
(girls). Surely you are already not doing right. I desired to see you
well-married while I was still living. But now I do not expect you to
be well-married to one (man). The father of the one with whom you
talk is evil. He (your lover) might beat you. That is the way his father
is. He is always beating his wife. And when anything is taking place,
he will not allow his wife to go there. Moreover, that man is extremely lazy. That is why I think the son will be like that. He is always merely walking around. I have never known him to do any
work. If you took him as your husband, you would probably then be
taking care of him. He would cheat you, for you already know how
to do all the work that belongs to us women. You really must not
take him for your husband. You must take the other one as your husband, the one with whom I think it proper for you to live. You must
stop talking with the one you are trying to love. If, however, I learn
that you talk again with him, you will cease to have control over any
of our things. I shall not believe anything you say to me. Now I
know in the past that you listened to what I told you. That is why I
believed you when you said anything to me. And this. As many
things as you have learned to make, I am very proud of (them). That
is why I would forbid you to go around with immoral (girls). Surely
as soon as you began to go around with them we found it out. You
are no longer afraid of men. You formerly were afraid to go
anywhere because of them. But now you always desire to go
somewhere. You will be thought of as naught if you are immoral.
The ones who are moral are those whom men want to live with (i.e.,
marry). And they will only make sport of the immoral ones. That is
why they bother them, to have a good time with them, not to marry
them. You might as well quickly take as your husband the one whom
I permit you," I was told.

I was nineteen years old. Then I made up my mind to begin talking with the one I was permitted. I did not like him very well. I thought more of the other one. Always I would think, "Would that I might talk (with him)." I really couldn't stop talking with him. I worried about him. And I again went around with the one I was permitted, when I went anywhere. Later on I became acquainted with him. But I always thought more of the other one, the one they hated on my account.

Soon the one I was permitted began to try to have me accompany him to his home. He always asked me to go with him whenever I saw him. Then I said to him, "I am very much afraid of your parents." "Well, I will go with you to your home," he said to me, "we do not speak a different language, so it is not right for us to be afraid of each other. As for me, I am not afraid of your parents. For I have done nothing evil to you. As long as we have been talking together, I have been quiet with you. You know it too. I intend that we shall live quietly with each other. I always think, 'Oh that she were willing.' You are the only one with whom I wish to live. I shall treat you very nicely. Whatever you tell me, I shall do. And I shall always work. And I shall not hate your parents. I am not fooling you. What I say to you this day, I shall surely do," he said to me. Soon I consented. At night we departed. When it was daylight, I was (rather) ashamed to go where we lived with him. The next day when he was seen, he surely was treated very nicely, for I had taken for a husband the one they had wished me to.

Then he gave me his horse, and the clothing which he used at dances, his finery. And I gave that horse to my brothers. Soon my mother-in-law came to summon me. "Go over there." my mother said to me. I departed. When I arrived there, "Right here," I was told. "Sit down," I was told. I sat down comfortably. Well, they began to clothe me in finery. I was clad all over in finery. Then, "You may also take this kettle (home)," I was told. There were also some dry goods in it, and a bridle was in the kettle. I had a very large bundle on my back when I departed. I arrived where we lived clad in finery. My mother looked at (the bundle). When she saw the bridle (she said), "Now you have two horses. If you had taken the other (man) as your husband, you wouldn't have been given anything." Soon I likewise was told, "I say, you take this (to them)." Food was placed in a sack, mattings (were to go), and several belts of yarn were tied around them. Then we were through (with the wedding ceremonies). And then only the relatives of my husband gave me each something, usually dry goods. And I would take a sack or basket full of food, beans, pumpkins (to his people), and mattings and corn.

Surely my husband for a long time treated me nicely. And my mother strongly forbade me to keep on talking with the other one. She watched me closely. But I couldn't stop thinking of him, for he was the one I loved. I did not love my husband. That is why I always thought of the other one. When anything was going on, I went around with my mother as she was watching me so that I should not talk with the other one again. And she forbade me to go any place by myself. "Go with your husband when you go any place. They might say something about you. Some one might say of you, 'she goes around with another man.' Those who desire to make trouble for married couples are smart," I would be told.

(At this time she had the baby as recounted in Chapter I.)

Then soon my husband began to act differently. He did not treat me at all the way he had done when he was acting nicely. The fact of the matter is that the young woman with whom I used to go around before I was married had been telling him something. "You are treating her so well, but your wife formerly was the same as married to another man. (That is) what I know about her. 'We shall never stop talking to each other even if we marry other (persons),' they said to each other," she kept on telling him. Finally he apparently really believed her. From that time on he began to treat me badly. That young woman was made jealous because he treated me well. That was why she kept on telling him stories. As for her, the men would not marry her as she was immoral. Finally (my husband) began to beat me.

"That is why I formerly forbade you to talk to any men. That is why I said to you. 'You must talk only to the one whom you are to marry,' " my mother said to me. "Finally you will make your son angry if you are always having trouble with each other. Babies die when they become angry." I was told.

And then later on (my husband) became meaner. He was lazy. But my mother forbade me to be divorced. And soon my mother died. I was twenty-five years old. I felt terribly. I remembered everything she told me from time to time.

And from that time I really began taking care of myself. It was very hard. Work never ended. (A person) could not just stay around (and do nothing). "Surely my mother treated me well in teaching me how to make things. What would have happened to me if I had not known work suitable for women? I should have been even poorer, if my mother had not instructed me," I thought all the while. Whenever I made anything I surely was given clothing to wear in exchange. And when I made something, I gave it away. In the spring when I planted anything I attended to it carefully. Surely I cooked it when it grew. In winter I did not lack things to cook.

And my husband did nothing but act meanly. When there was a dance he would not allow me to go and see it. Soon I thought, "Well, now that my mother has gone, this fellow treats me meanly. It was because my mother forbade me to become a divorcée that (I allowed) this fellow to ill-treat me. Besides I do not love him. Now no one would scold me. And I love the other one. I hate this one." I began to see dances in spite (of what he had said). He was fearfully angry. "It's because you may see that man is why you are perverse in going there," he said to me. "I want to see him," I would say to him. I began to chase him away.

"You may marry other (women) who are quiet (i.e., moral). We shall never be able to live nicely together. While I was living quietly (i.e., morally) with you, you began to act badly. And it was not my idea to live with you. It was because I was told. I suppose I was permitted so that you would treat me well and not abuse me. So now we will be divorced. You must go. You could have behaved nicely if you had wished us to live together always. You might have been working quietly so that we should not be poor. You know how I have been doing. I have been working quietly. And you without reason began to be jealous. I have not talked to any one as long as we have been living together. But now we must surely be divorced," I said to him.

"Truly from now on I shall stop acting that way. I shall begin to treat you nicely. And I shall work diligently. I shall not be able to refuse what you ask me. From now on you shall have control of what we shall continue to do,'' he said to me. "No, I shall not believe you though you may do your best to speak nicely. You have ill-treated me too long,'' I said to him. I was not able to chase him away. As I was leaving he came and seized me. "Believe me,'' he said to me. "No, indeed,'' I said to him. He held me there. "You are not going off any place,'' he said to me. I cried bitterly and he let me go.

I went where my uncle (mother's brother) lived and slept there. The next day my uncle said to me, "It is strange that you came and slept with us. Something has happened to you.'' "My husband treats me very badly. That is why I was unwilling (to keep on living with him),'' I said to him. "It is known broadcast that he abuses you. No one will reproach you if you think of being divorced. I myself will not scold you. It is a rule that a married couple should alike treat each other well. As for me, I treat the one with whom I live (i.e., wife) well and she treats me well. She always cooks for me when I am working. And if I were suddenly to treat her badly while she was still treating me well and while she was still living morally, were I to become jealous over something without reason, her relatives would not like it. For I surely would be doing wrong. If she cast me off none of her relatives would scold her. Every one, all over, would be glad of what happened to me. Certainly I should not find one (woman) who behaved as well. Surely I should always want back the one who behaved well. (But) I might have angered her. I alone should be thinking of her. Surely she would not think of me. She would hate me as much as possible,'' my uncle said to me. "Well, my niece (sister's daughter), now you are of sufficient age to listen attentively,'' he said to me. "You probably still think of what your mother told you. You may foolishly begin to be immoral. You should look at men quietly (i.e., without an immoral purpose). Whomever you think will treat you well is the one whom you should take for your husband. If he happens to treat you well, you should live quietly with him. Do not again desire another (husband). For it also is not right for you women to have many husbands. A woman who does that is gossiped about a good deal. It is the same as if she goes from man to man. That, my niece, is what I want you to do. Because your mother is gone is why I tell you as I understand it. And if you are now divorced you should stay (single) for at least one or two years. You should just be working diligently. Then you might marry that one,'' my uncle said to me.

And so I became divorced. Of course (my former husband) was always trying to get me, but I could not be kind again to him. I hated him tremendously.

And the wife of the (man) with whom I talked when I was still a virgin died. After I had been divorced for one year and he had become a widower free from death-customs, he again began to (court) me. Of course others courted me but I did not talk to them. And soon I began talking with him, for we were already acquainted with each other while we were young. And soon he asked me why I became divorced. I told him exactly how it was that I became divorced.

''Well! He was entirely wrong in what he thought of us. I ceased seeing you when you were married. Even if I had seen you I should not have been able to screw up my courage to say anything to you. You surely would have reported me. You acted that way when you were married. If I had persuaded you (to marry me) at the time, I should not have beaten you. Now you must be willing for us to do that,'' he said to me. ''I suppppose you too will beat me, that is why you are courting me,'' I said to him. ''Why, how often have you heard of me striking the one with whom I was living? I never struck her even once. Nor did I scold her. She danced vigorously at dances also before she became ill. That is how I should treat you too. You might dance vigorously if you felt like dancing vigorously. To dance vigorously is natural. I do not know of any one being married (at the dances). How, pray, could any one act in a courting way as there would be many people? No one would fail to be seen if he courted there. I should think that way myself. If you are willing we shall do that. I want you to consent very much. I have always thought, 'I wish I might live with her,' '' he said to me. ''Well, I might consent in a year, but not now,'' I said to him. For a long time we were merely talking with each other.

The one with whom I formerly lived never gave up. He always tried to court me. But I could not think kindly of him again. For he had angered me as he already had treated me badly. I hated him thoroughly.

Soon the time came which I had set for us to live together. When we saw each other, he said to me, "Well, at last it is the time you set for your consent. To-night at night do not latch your door firmly. I shall come to you." That is what I did. He came. And sometimes he would sleep far off in a wickiup where his relatives lived. And at any time I went and visited my relatives. He never spoke crossly to me. So I loved him dearly. The other one, the one with whom I first lived, was sensual. That is why I hated him.

The Morals of the Aricara

The Aricara Indians lived along the Missouri River in what is now South Dakota, and their villages became regular stops for traders during the fur trade era of the early nineteenth century. This selection is from the journal of a French trader who lived among the Aricara in 1803-04. In light of what you have already read of Indian morality, how perceptive do you think this white man's observations are? (Annie H. Abel, ed., Tabeau's Narrative of Loisel's Expedition to the Upper Missouri *(1939), 174-82.)*

As for the Ricara women, I have reason to believe that it is, in derision or in irony, that some travelers have called them the Circassians of the Missouri or else the present race has degenerated greatly. This is difficult to believe on seeing the old women. They are certainly the most ugly and have the advantage of surpassing all the others in slovenliness. They generally have a color as of death, as far as one can judge through the layers of dirt, in which sweat or the rain has traced lines. And I would not be accused of exaggeration here, if decency did not forbid a detail, too repugnant. I shall say only that, after having eaten almost a year with the Ricaras, one ought not to be allowed to be fastidious or disgusted.

The clothing of the Ricaras is: One cannot be more unadorned. They are naked and wear carelessly over the shoulder a robe or a dressed skin. Leggings of antelope-skin and shoes of buffalo hide are worn, in summer, only at ceremonies and, in winter, for protection from the cold, to which habit has rendered these Savages almost insensible. The 17th. of December, when it was 26° below zero, many, quite naked, played, at daybreak upon the ice, a game that the French have called billiards without it having the least resemblance to our game. The Savages are passionately fond of this game; but, although it gives much exercise, the weather was hardly suitable for this amusement and, as I thought I saw that there was bragging, I judged that they paid somewhat dear for the renown of man above pain. Perhaps, all these old partisans of physical impassiveness would have hesitated about giving a proof of their system in this way.

The women are covered with a skin of the cow or of the doe, bound around the middle of the body, sewed on the two sides, and ornamented with long fringes at the bottom and down the seams. They wear, also leggings of antelope-skin. They cover the shoulders and the upper part of the arms with two kinds of wings. From the elbow to the wrist the sleeve is very narrow and is also ornamented with threads, which are everywhere a great adornment. The blue bead, as precious here as the porcelain among the nations of the Mississippi, is used to trim all the seams of these sacks called Roman by some Frenchmen. The Sioux women are dressed almost in the same fashion and are distinguished only by rolls of brass wire in the ears and by huge locks of hair, covered with blue beads and tied on the temples in the shape of cushions.

The Sioux women, although not very strict, are more reserved than the Ricara women. It could be said that the latter do justice to themselves and know the value of their favors, if their facility in granting them is any criterion. The most inflexible is not proof against a prize of vermilion and of twenty strands of blue beads. There are, nevertheless, a few prudes who greatly wish to pass for cautious ones; but who surrender themselves, moreover, with discretion and secrecy. All are generally hostile to ceremony and, to avoid the embarrassment of an intrigue, they ordinarily make the first advances in a less equivocal manner and it is here where one truly takes the romance by the tail. The most peculiar thing is that all goes on often in the presence of and even by order of a jealous husband. This paradox will be no longer a paradox when it is understood that a Sioux, as a Ricara, is alive to this affront only when his wife, by a secret infidelity, departs from his house. Therefore, all that which meets with his approval, being in order, is not offensive and such a man, who would kill or at least turn out his wife upon the slightest suspicion, prostitutes her himself for a very small reward and it is seen that a wife has not yet been chastised for having failed in submission in like case.

I have seen among the Bois Brulés a secret infidelity punished and a husband order his wife to be unfaithful. Here are the two cases: The 6th. of August a man surprises his better half in flagrant wrong-doing and, in order to avoid all proceedings, he takes it upon himself to pronounce and to execute sentence. He commences by removing her hair from the nape of the neck up to brow and, stopping near the ears, he allows the hair and skin to hang down each side. He continues his work by mutilating her arms and hands and ends by a cut of the knife on the shoulder-blade. The wife having wholly recovered from the wounds, he said that if she did wrong again he would regard her as incorrigible. A Savage regards the infidelity of his wife in favor of a white man less of a sin, in that she is won by the allurement of gain and he does not dream that this rival presumes to think that he is preferred to himself. This opinion, elsewhere, is perhaps often the hidden cause of jealousy and it cannot be otherwise among the Savages, who know neither love nor delicacy.

A Sioux brave, wishing to prove that he is brave-hearted, comes, in open daylight, to find a Frenchman at the Isle of Cedars. He is followed by his young wife, one of the prettiest of the village and, moreover, reputed discreet. He offers the favors of this well-beloved, demanding only a few small articles in return. The cavalier, although surprised, is not the man to give up his cloak and offers at first a fine knife, a prize of vermilion, and about six inches of tobacco. As the present appeared small because of her attractions, the husband pulls off the robe in which the Venus is wrapped through modesty and, in spite of some affected manners, increased, of course, the price of his goods by exposing it. The cavalier still hesitated, when the victim to whom the sacrifice was doubtless painful, but who feared, never-theless, to lose the occasion of proving her submissiveness, remarked that knives with a green handle were not common; that the vermilion was a beautiful red; that the tobacco—in short, well, what else? At least, she speaks so well that they agree and the husband firmly holds the door.

This politeness is carried out every day among the Ricaras, and always the more readily in the case of the whites; but infidelities, unavowed, are not always punished severely and the braves ordinarily content themselves with repudiating the wives. This is, often, only a momentary divorce. Besides, the intrigues are so common that they are generally made light of. Furthermore, reciprocation of injury suffices in a nation, where immodesty is carried to its highest pitch.

The word, modesty, is not even known among the Ricaras. The Chayennes and the Caninanbiches are reserved in this respect, even in their conversation. The Sioux are, at least, modestly covered; but the Ricara men are absolutely nude. Through force of habit, though, no notice is taken of it. The women and the young girls mingle with the men and laugh, inconsequently, at the most obscene things. The men, nevertheless, would think it immodest to be without a loin cloth made of blades of curled grass. To neglect this is here a great fault. The 2nd. of August I saw all the women and girls of the village, spectators of a comic dance, where the men, attached thus, two by two, drew backwards and offered, in their gambols, attitudes which drew great applause. After that, it would surely astonish one to hear it said that the girls are virtuous before marriage and that there are virgins, eighteen to twenty years old. Truth exceeds probability here. It is true that the mothers and all the relatives watch with the greatest care and that they carry watchfulness up to the point of fastening at night the petticoats of the girls who lie thus tied down. Nevertheless, these bonds are not proof against a lover who pleases; but, according to their law, that is a marriage and, even if it last only an hour, the girl becomes, none the less, an honest widow.

Incest is not recognized till the third degree and the brother and the sister in my lodge are considered to be beyond criticism. It is needful to confess that they save appearances as much as they can. The seventy-year old man and his eldest sister, being unable, doubtless, to find better fortune elsewhere, mutually gratify themselves. It does not appear that there is much to say about it. Incest, on the contrary, seems infinitely applicable to the son-in-law, who often marries all the sisters and, were his mother-in-law a hundred years old, he would fail in good manners and filial respect if, from time to time, he did not secretly gratify the old woman.

Women are of so little importance among the Sioux and the

Ricaras that it would be astonishing if the husbands were fastidious about their conduct from any other motive than that which I have already explained. They are, in the fullest sense, slaves; for, being bought, they become property that the husband can lend, give away, and sell when it pleases him. A Ricara lost at play the enjoyment of his wife for some days and he lay tranquilly at the foot of the bed, while the young man who had won received, in his sight, a thousand caresses. I know not if this was in order to be revenged on her husband or to pay honestly his debt; but she did reproach him for being a great gambler and she made much more fuss the next morning over a basket he had lost in play.

A monster, whom I looked upon every day with horror, had a pretty wife. He learns that she is unfaithful to him and, to hide his plan of vengeance, he says many times to his friends, that repeatedly in his dreams the French demand his wife of him. The barbarian, at length, takes her aside one day and, after having stabbed her, dismembers her and sacrifices her limbs to the French and the four points of the compass. He then carries the tongue to the village and coolly tells of his execrable crime. The relatives murmured at first; one spoke of vengeance; but everything is easily quieted. What could one say? She was his wife and he could dispose of her.

The women do not assist at any ceremony and are not present at the feasts where the husbands alone eat greedily all that which the women are able to procure. In their lodge even, they do not always taste the daily fare which is divided generally among the masters, the guests, and the parasites. They have, none the less, charge of the cooking. This is not displeasing to them as this is their only opportunity of approaching the fire which they replenish. There is in these lodges an insupportable cold as there is in the center only a single fire of little dried sticks, always surrounded by men crowded together, who prevent heat passing beyond and reaching the women behind them.

The Ricara women appear to endure their hardships with more fortitude than the Sioux whom their hard lot often drives to suicide. I saw many cases of suicide during the six months I lived on the Isle of Cedars. A young woman hanged herself; some days after, a very pretty girl followed her example; a third did likewise; but her mother, who suspected her plan, arrived soon enough to save her by cutting the rope. It is always this kind of death that they choose and they are often found strangled without being suspended, madness giving them the courage to draw, until death comes, upon the cord tied to a tree.

The venereal disease makes terrible ravages here and, from the moment it attacks a man, it makes more progress in eight days than elsewhere in five or six weeks.

IV. WORK AND PLAY

There were not a great variety of occupations among Indian societies. Consequently, both work and play were highly formalized, with strictly enforced rules to determine the eligibility for a certain kind of work or game. What were some of those rules? Why do you think such rules existed? What was the general pattern of the sexual division of labor? When an Indian man or woman undertook a particular task, how free were they to do the job in the way they wished? Why? What impact has the introduction of European technology had on Indian work? Was their technology adequate for the Indian way of life?

Work Among the Ojibwa

The Ojibwa Indians lived west of Lake Superior in Minnesota and southern Canada. This passage describes their labor system. (Ruth Landes, The Ojibwa Woman, *125-30.)*

Women are given little consideration culturally. To women are allotted the quiet, sedentary, and domestic occupations that are not considered dependent upon supernatural gifts. This neglect is bolstered by the belief that women, because of their harmful blood discharges, must be kept from contact with the bountiful supernaturals. One noted shaman went so far as to say that his supernatural "brother" dreaded a woman's bloomers as symbols of sex and maleficence.

Prescriptively feminine work is extremely varied. It is learned and practised by every girl, no matter to what extent she may supplement it with male work. She sets simple twine traps about the wigwam to catch whatever small creatures may wander into them; these are usually rabbits. She does this regularly, and it is the first lesson in trapping which she teaches her children. The snared rabbit is skinned, the meat and bones thrown into the cooking pot, the fur saved for weaving into rabbit robes. These robes are pretty and warm, and invaluable to hunters. The woman cuts the fur of one rabbit into a long, thin, continuous rope, which is tied onto another such rope made from the fur of another rabbit; one rope is then used in the weaving as weft, and another rope as warp. They use long strips of grass and cedar bark for weaving also, and make mats out of them to be used on the floor or stood up against the lodge wall. Native or commercial twine is used to crochet fishnets used by women and men.

Women tan deer and moose hides in several different ways, to produce varying grades of fineness and coarseness in texture, and colors that range from brownish tan to a yellowish cream. The desired texture and color are determined by the use to which the hide will be put. Moccasins for serviceable wear are made of a leather that is tanned to a rich tan color and to a coarse thick texture, whereas moccasins used at dances are made of leather as delicate and pretty as a European's kid glove.

Women used to do all the tailoring and sewing, but this work has been displaced partially by commercial products. They still make moccasins and the bead-embroidered "aprons" men wear at native dances. An "apron" is a huge pocket for a man's tobacco, flint or matches, and pipe, slung under one arm by long straps which cross over the opposite shoulder. A well-outfitted dancer wears a pair of such aprons. Some women in the hinterland still make hide garments for their men, cut however after the fashion of European garments. They also make mitts and caps of muskrat hide and fur. In olden times, the women made a long shirt, loin cloth, leggings, and a sort of wind-break rabbit blanket for the men; for themselves they made an extra-long shirt or dress with attachable sleeves held in place by draw strings, shorter leggings than those worn by the men, and a rabbit blanket. "People were never sick in those days. They did not get sick until they commenced wearing White clothes, and the men began to cut their hair." Today many women tailor calico and serge garments for themselves and their young children. They also clean and mend their husband's garments and adornments. This is quite a gesture among the Ojibwa, for ordinarily the rigid separateness of individuals extends as well to their possessions. The husband generally does not reciprocate this gesture, however.

The "moss-back" cradles in which infants are carried, or were carried until lately, are made in two stages, one of which is men's work and the other women's. The husband makes the wooden frame, the wife makes the leather sack or blanket which is sewn onto the frame, and is laced around the infant. The leather of the sack is now being replaced by velvet, as being more modish. Snowshoes are likewise made in two stages. The man makes the wooden frame, and his wife or sister or mother weaves or crochets the rawhide (usually moose hide) mesh.

Women of the backwoods still manufacture their own needles and thread, or did until very recently. The needle is made of a marten's penis-bone, or sometimes of tough wood. The thread is made from the long back tendons of moose and deer, sometimes from the tendons of dead horses, occasionally from buffalo tendons, whenever a buffalo strayed into the woods for shelter and was caught there. The tendons are prepared by separating out the component threads, which are then stretched and dried; "and they never break." Some plant products are also used as sewing thread, especially for binding together bark blankets and utensils.

Some women still prepare native vegetable dyes, though these are being increasingly supplemented by commercial products. The native colors are brilliant and fast. They were used chiefly for coloring porcupine quills which were then sewn onto deer hide in blocks that formed geometrical designs of triangles, diamonds, and squares. I have seen specimens of these natively dyed quills that are about a half-century old and which still sparkle though the quills themselves are partly broken, the commercial thread is rotten, and the hide is grey with age. In these old pieces, the native colors were a deep orange-scarlet, a gleaming yellow that darkened occasionally into light orange, and a deep violet or purple. There were also a dark pink and a light bluish green which the Indians consider commercial, but which they think had native analogues.

Women used to embroider hide garments and moccasins with porcupine quill work. Some women still know how to prepare the quills and how to sew them on. The quills are plucked out of a freshly killed porcupine, and steeped in hot water for several days until they become pliable. The quills, which are normally ovoid and resistant, are then easily flattened out by applying pressure with the thumb nail. They are dipped in the dyes, and left to dry. When used in embroidery, the quill is placed in a vertical position and each end is passed over and under a fine thread loop.

Quill work has been supplanted by the far simpler bead work. The use of beads was concomitant with the introduction of curvilinear designs. The old geometric designs have almost entirely disappeared with the disappearance of the quill technique. In beadwork, a varying number of beads are strung on a thread and tacked down with a stitch at intervals. This is an entirely different technique from that employed in the quill work. Embroidery in silks is also popular, and is handled like beadwork.

Until recently, women made a number of utensils out of birchbark. These included implements for cooking, eating, and storing. The sides were sewn together with native thread, and handles were attached in the same way. Large, relatively decorative spoons were made of wood. Hunters still resort to bark and wood utensils. Bark utensils used to be decorated by the women. They would bite into the fresh bark, and with their teeth imprint geometrical and curvilinear designs. This is now a lost art.

Birchbark is also used for roofing. This bark is indispensable to the wigwam. It is waterproof, breaks the winds, and is easily portable. Women roll large sheets of it off the tree in early summer, toughen it before the fire and in the sun, correct uneven and weak spots, and sew sheets together end to end to make an ample blanket for the roof.

Women pick berries and cherries throughout the summer months: strawberries, blueberries, gooseberries, chokecherries. Curiously, they are not interested in raspberries. They cook all this fruit and eat it as a simple boiled dish, pour it into soup, eat it with meat or wild rice or fish, and recently have learned to make fruit pies. They also dry the fruit, storing it for future use in the fall and winter. The Ojibwa who neighbor the Cree also make pemmican, and chop dried fruit up with the meat.

Women harvest and preserve aquatic rice, assisted by their husbands. A man poles the canoe while his wife harvests the grain. Each woman spreads her rice on the ground upon a bark spread, or upon a rack, to dry in the sun. Then it is placed upon a rack over a fire, to cure in the thick smoke. The husband then treads the rice, to loosen the husks; then his wife fans the trodden rice. When it is prepared, it is stored in a fawnskin sack.

Women assume the principal role in sugar-making. Most of the maple-sugar groves are owned in the name of some woman. The entire family goes to the sugar groves. A woman, her husband, and her grown children who are as yet unmarried choose certain trees upon which to work alone. Each person drives a cut into a tree and places a pan at the base of the tree to receive the sugar sap. When the pans are full of sap, they are emptied into great kettles or tubs near the wigwam. The woman places the tubs over great fires, and vigorously stirs the sap with a paddle while it boils. Each tub of sap is treated somewhat differently, depending upon its ultimate use as syrup, ground sugar, or block sugar. For example, the sap intended for syrup does not boil as long as that designed for ground sugar, more water is poured into it, it is stirred more, and the fire is not so fierce.

Every woman sets out nets for fish, especially during the seasons of open water. Fish is used for the lighter meals, such as breakfast, also to tide over shortages in the meat supply, or to add variety to the diet. It is considered a most important item. The large organs of some large fish are used as storing utensils; oil, for instance, was formerly stored in sturgeon bladders.

A woman often aids her husband in his hunting. While the husband does the actual shooting, she handles the canoe on duck or moose hunts, and is on the watch for game and for signs of danger. She also performs part of the sacrifices her husband must offer after a successful bear or moose hunt. She cleans the skull of the bear, paints it "prettily" in red and blue circles and stripes, adorns it with bright colored ribbons, slings a small sack of tobacco about it, and hangs it on some tree. She handles the "bell" of the moose head with the same respect, adorns it with ribbons, and hangs it aloft with a sack of tobacco.

The woman cures fish and meat in different ways. Fish secured in winter, and meat also, if there is a surplus, is hung on racks to be frozen, and this weathering alone preserves it. In summer and early fall fish is cured by exposure to sun and smoke. Jerked meat is treated in the same way, but the process may continue through the winter.

Women gather herbs for food and medicinal purposes. The food herbs are chiefly tea-substitutes; they are less in demand now than in earlier days. However each woman is still busily occupied collecting medicinal herbs, of which a great variety are employed. The bark of certain trees is used as medicament and nourishment during times of winter starvation.

Herbal doctoring is practised by both men and women. That is, women do not become eligible for the profession as a simple consequence of their sex; but those who are vitally interested in the work apply themselves to it continuously, and the gifted ones are recognized and are in constant demand by patients. The native pharmacopoeia is remarkably extensive; besides herbs, it includes animal products such as bear gall and certain skunk secretions. There are numerous traditional prescriptions for a great variety of ailments, and new prescriptions seem to be invented daily. Pharmaceutics is the interest of older, rather than of young women; or it may be that older women have become distinguished through long practise. Middle-aged women spend days grubbing in the soil, and return laden with branches and roots. Their wigwams are hung with sacks containing these materials, waiting for the occasion to be brewed into a prescription. Some women are so interested that they trade with individuals in distant groups of Cree, Dakota, etc., to secure herbs that are not indigenous.

Women are the midwives of the Ojibwa. Men are excluded from a childbirth except for a certain brief magical performance which is resorted to in a desperate case. Midwifery is a highly skilled occupation, depending upon an extensive herbal knowledge, detailed knowledge of the female anatomy and physiology, varied massage techniques, and a cool and resourceful intelligence. This profession, too, is not open to all women but only to those who show marked aptitude and interest. Public recognition of a woman's ability is expressed by repeated requests for her services at confinements.

Women, together with children and disabled older men, are important as a chorus to the exploits of the warriors. As the men leave for the war-path, the women are supposed to escort them part way in canoes, cheering them on with songs that promise victory, referring to old conquests, reminding them of unsatisfied grievances against the Sioux, deriding the Sioux. If the warriors return successful, the women are notified of the fact by the men's songs of conquest, and paddle out in a welcoming body, to greet them with songs and cheers and to snatch the enemy scalps. If the warriors return defeated, the women are again notified by the dirges that the men sing, and they remain ashore, singing a mournful response.

Women continually make artistic contributions which are much appreciated, but which are given no formal recognition. Artistic women—in marked contrast to gifted men—are given no title nor are they regarded with the awe that indicates general respect. Many of the native love songs which are immensely popular, known over several localities, and passed down for several generations, have been composed by women. Songs are composed quite spontaneously by women while at their work; they are overheard by others who repeat and add to them, and they are gradually added more or less permanently to the cultural stock. Not much less than one hundred years ago, Two Seated Woman composed a song in quite a homely fashion at her work. Her lover had departed for a time, and missing him, she hummed about him:

> "Now I start to weep.
> My lover went away.
> Without him how will I cross
> When I come to the Path-leading-to-the-river?
>
> He told me, my lover,
> 'Don't cry, don't,
> When I depart for the Path-leading-to-the-river.
> Do not worry, do not mind.'
>
> Indeed, I will follow him.
> To the Path-leading-to-the-river he went.
> But indeed, how will I cross
> When I come to the Path-leading-to-the-river?
>
> Ah-h-h, then I will see my lover."

Apache Horse-raiding

This passage is the story of a Jicarilla Apache's first participation in the warfare that was typical of many Indian tribes. How would you describe the conduct of the raid—disciplined or disorganized? (Opler, Childhood and Youth in Jicarilla Apache Society, *142-47.)*

At this time there were five of us living together. I had two sisters, a mother, and a father. My sisters were single. I had two older brothers, but they both got married and went away. In those days poor people had to go on foot. Very few had horses. We had to carry big loads wherever we went. I got tired of carrying loads on my back all the time.

I had a friend my age. He heard that some men were going out raiding. He came to me. He said, "When the people move camp, I have to carry a load on my back. I'm tired of it."

I told him, "I'll go with you on that raiding party." Then I told him, "My friend, listen carefully. Note what day the men are going. When they go we must run after them."

We were both untaught. We didn't know it was not the way to do.

I went around to visit. I heard that in two days they were going to have a war dance and that whoever wanted to join the raid was supposed to dance.

The next day my friend came to me and said, "Tomorrow the people are going to haul wood to the place where the dance will take place."

My father had two brothers. My father's sisters were three, and I had one mother's brother. My mother had two sisters. But I didn't let them know that I was going to join the raiding group. None of my relatives had horses. I looked at horses, and they looked pretty to me. I was just wishing for them all the time.

My friend brought messages to me all the time. He kept urging me to go. He said, "Let's go! Then we can ride all the time and will not have to carry packs on our backs."

I was excited, for that fellow came around to me every day. The day of the dance he said, "This evening you must paint your face and dress in good clothes and join that dance, for when a person joins the dance, he can't back out."

When I got home my mother was making corn meal mush. She gave some to my father to eat and some to me.

After supper my father told me, "Now get ready. Paint your face."

I asked my father, "With what paint shall we paint our faces?" And my father said, "There is some red paint."

Then I asked him, "Do all paint the face the same?"

And my father answered. "No, those who are dancing [i.e., those who are going on the raid] paint themselves with red and black and white paint and have their faces streaked with it."

Then I said to my father, "I'm going to see my friend. I'm going to the dance with him."

I went over to my friend and found him already painted. His face was painted white and black and red. So I painted myself the same way.

By that time the singing had started. The four men with the drum were there singing, facing the east. The raid leader began first and danced alone for one song. Then the next song was started, and the others began to come out. After five men had come out there, my friend and I went out. We danced and others joined us. Twenty-eight came out altogether. They came out with stone axes, spears, bows and arrows, with weapons of all kinds. My friend and I had nothing but clubs made of wood. We danced all night.

Daylight came. The dance was over. The twenty-eight men stood aside. Then the leader told us, "Line up and face the north." He walked back and forth along the line of men four times. He said, "All right! I like all you men who want to go. You two boys are all right. It's all right that you carried clubs in your hands when you danced. If you had carried nothing in your hands, you could not go along with us. Those clubs kill people too."

Then the leader gave advice to the men. "Get your arrows and ropes and provisions of pounded meat ready. After two days we will start out."

When I got home all my relatives came around and scolded me severely. My father nearly whipped me. He said, "You have never trained for such a long journey. You have never trained to go without sleep, without food." They scolded me and called me a fool. But I remained quiet. All that day they scolded me, but I said no word.

Early the next morning, before daybreak, my father woke me up. He said, "Tell both your brothers to come and see me."

I went and told them. They both came. My uncle and aunt came too.

My father said, "You must help this boy. You, his brothers, must give him a good bow and arrows and a quiver. You know he has been dancing with those men, though he has never been trained to be tough, and I don't know why he joined that dance!"

Then my father spoke to the women. "Each one of you sew some moccasins for him. Make the soles double thickness. Have three pairs altogether."

And he said to my brothers, "You must make a rope for him." My oldest brother had a rope for me.

My mother parched some corn by putting it in a pan over the fire and ground it. At sunset all was ready.

When the sun set I went to my friend's place to see how he was getting along. He was ready too, but his father was still scolding him.

When I came back my father began to tell me all about the hard times on the raid. He said, "I'm your father, but I didn't send you on this raid. It is your own decision. After they paint you with white clay you can't speak in the ordinary way. You may have to go without water and food for four days. You must not cry or ask for help. If you fall from the horse because you are so tired, you must not cry."

In the morning someone came and told me, "You must be ready by noon."

I went to tell my friend. Halfway he met me and he told me the same thing. My friend said, "This morning my father was still scolding me. I think he's just telling lies. He's telling how hard it is. The way it looks to me, we should have a good time walking and seeing new territory and things. My bundle is all ready."

My brother had given me a good quiver and many good arrows. Before noon I started with my equipment and bundle to see my friend, for it was nearly time to start. My friend sent over his younger brother to see whether the men were ready. The boy came back and said that the men were gathering and were all ready. My bundle was not very heavy; it felt light. It was not like carrying heavy camp possessions as I had to do every time camp was broken.

We went over to the place where there was a big crowd of people. When we got there the leader started to walk. They had been waiting for us. We traveled all day long. We went till the middle of the night and stopped to sleep.

The next morning four men sat to the side. When the leader said, "Let's go," four more joined them, and these eight left for home. There were still twenty of us. We passed the mountain where white clay is obtained, and the next morning we were painted with white clay. Two others were painted first and then my companion and I. Ten others changed their minds at this point and didn't want to be painted with clay.

The leader was angry now. He pointed to us two and said, "You'd better go back with these ten people. You'll change your minds too!" We didn't say a word.

He spoke to the others, the ten. "Now go back to your own country."

We faced the east. The leader said, "Do not say a word in your own language." We passed the last mountains and woods. Then four more backed out and spoke their own language and said, "We are going back." Now there were only six left.

The leader tried to speak to us but we didn't say a word. Now the six of us started on. The leader gave us advice and taught us how to act on the raid. He said, "You'd better not look to the side or behind."

Then about noon he started to run. We thought he was just going to run for a little way, but he ran all afternoon. I asked my friend, "Are you tired?" He was still fresh. I was not tired either. That night the leader just kept running all night long, but I did not tire. I said to my friend, "Are you tired?" He was all right too.

At sunrise we got to the river. We ate our food there. We all said, "I put down the wolf's paw," and put down our food. We sat around in a circle and ate. Our water bags made of intestines were dry, so we put them in the water to soak, because they keep water cooler when they are soaked. We refilled them with water too. Then we started off.

We traveled all day. All that night we traveled, but my companion and I were not sleepy. We were out in the Plains country. We found a big hole where the buffalo had lain. There was grass growing in the hole at this time.

The leader said, "You must crawl in this grass and sleep here all day."

We slept and didn't know that the sun had set. Someone woke me up and woke up my friend too. The leader told us to come. We went a little way walking. As soon as we were warmed up we started to run. We ran all night until the morning glow showed. About noon we brought out our food again and said, "I put down the wolf's paw." It was the last of the provisions we had brought along. After eating, we started on again. We had many restrictions. We could look only to the front; we couldn't even look down.

The leader said, "We are almost there. Tonight we'll start back for our own country." I was very glad to hear that.

This was mostly level country. We came in sight of some hills, though. Then the leader told us, "You must lie here in the tall grass. I'm going to get on top of that hill."

I didn't understand the language of the leader, but the men told me what he meant. He got to the top of the hill and looked over. Then he dropped down and rolled down the hill to us again. He said he had seen lots of camps and people. The five of us were lying down together. The leader lay down far apart from us.

It was just getting dark when we heard some voices behind us. We couldn't understand and we didn't look, for we weren't supposed to look around. Then some enemies passed, carrying buffalo meat. We acted as if we were paying no attention, but the leader knew what was going on. The leader said, "Do not pay attention. Do not be afraid. They are deaf and blind. We are going back tonight."

Then he told us, "Get your ropes ready. I'm going to get horses." And he left for the enemy camps.

The leader went out to the east. In about half an hour he came driving many horses. He drove them to us and then said, "Come on, but drive them slowly!" We did.

In a little while he said, "Get your spears and worn-out moccasins and put them on a sloping place." The spear I had wasn't mine, but was one that had been lent to me, yet I had to do it.

The leader walked around the horses sunwise. The leader always does this. Then he said, "Now rope your horses. I have put a fence around them."

I was the last one to get a horse. Now we were freed of restrictions. We could use our own language. A smoky-colored horse faced me. I roped it. He had some bells around his neck. I didn't know for sure that he was a good horse. It was too dark to see. When I got on, it was just as though he had a saddle on, he was so fat. He was a good one.

The leader said, "Let us drive them slowly. The enemy might hear us."

After we had gone two miles he spoke to us again. He said, "You all have grandfathers and grandmothers. Perhaps you have had good training from them, so you won't fall from the horses and will act like men."

We drove the horses all day and all night. We went fast. The next day we traveled all day. We kept going until the middle of the night. Some colts were getting tired. We shot them with arrows, for when you leave them behind the enemy can use them to go after you. We traveled all night and all the next morning.

The leader said, "Let's kill a colt." We found some wood.

When the colt was killed I cut a strip of hide about three inches wide from the hide. I made a hole at each end and put my feet in each end and used it for stirrups. I put it over the horse's back; I was sitting right over it.

After we had eaten, the leader said, "Let's go, or they will follow us."

We started off and traveled all day and all night too. The next morning we were near the mountains. We got on top, to the spring. This was the trail the people traveled. About noon we passed the Canadian River. That night it was moonlight so we kept on traveling. Before midnight we got home.

Many of the horses we had brought were wild, so we put the horses in a rough corral near the camp. All of us got on horseback and started to our homes then, leaving most of the horses behind in the corral, not far from the camps.

Everyone woke up when I got home. My father was very happy. He held that horse for me. He had not believed I was coming home again.

The next day we divided the horses. I took fifteen. I gave two horses to my father and two to my mother, one to each of my older brothers, for they had helped me out; to my other relatives I gave the rest—all but three which I saved for myself.

The Potlatch

The Indians of the northwest Pacific coast practiced a custom which is unique in human society. What was the purpose of the "potlatch"? How was it conducted? Do you know of any practice in modern America which is similar in form or function? The following description was made in the 1890s by an Indian agent of the Canadian government. (William M. Halliday, Potlatch and Totem and the Recollections of an Indian Agent *(1935), 73-80.)*

When arrangements were all completed, two messengers were sent round bidding all the people to come, and as every one present knew that there was an unusual amount to be given away, and that each share would therefore be large accordingly, but would also entail a corresponding liability on the part of the receivers, no one could willingly be absent, so that the crowd was exceptionally large.

When they were all assembled, Awalaskinis himself took the floor and addressed the people. 'Friends, chiefs, and nobles of the various tribes gathered here! I want you all to know that I am now about to give away to all of you so much that no other chief has ever eclipsed me in the matter of giving. You all know that my generosity is very great towards you all. I have feasted and fed you now for some weeks, as becomes a great chief, but that sinks into insignificance beside what I am about to do. You will all remember my benevolence as long as you live, and you will also remember the great value of all that I am now about to give. To-day, according to the custom of our fathers and forefathers, I am about to distribute a portion of the *howanaka*, and had I not been such a great chief, and allied with such a great chief as Weetsikok, I could never have hoped to accomplish what I am now about to do.'

The young men then came forward and gifts of button blankets, silk handkerchiefs, and clothing were distributed to each and every person present, according to clan. The first to receive were the eagle clan of the Kwawkewlths, then the whale clan, next the wolf, last the grizzly bear. These constituted the clans of that tribe in order of precedence. The Mamlillikullas followed according to clans, and so on down the line until each individual had received his portion. The chief of each clan made a short speech on behalf of himself and his clan, all in turn stating what a great chief Awalaskinis was, and how pleased they were to partake of his hospitality. For each speech made by a chief an extra blanket was given him. All the speeches, however, were not eulogistic. Kakanus, of the Mamtagu branch of one of the tribes, was very angry.

'I came here at the invitation of Awalaskinis. It had been told me that he was a great chief and a very generous one. I came willingly, that I might partake of his hospitality, and at the same time receive payment from him for what I gave him at my *potlatch*. Instead of his giving me five blankets with interest thereon, he has only given me three, and I fail to see why he should be called great or generous. I call him only a third-rater.'

This complaint and several others of a similar nature were, however, amicably adjusted by extra gifts being given to the grumblers, but the harmony of the gathering was considerably disturbed, and it grew worse as the days went on.

When three of the tribes had received their portions, there was a brief pause, and Awalaskinis stood up before the whole crowd with his speaker's staff in his hand, and rapped four times to draw the attention of the people to himself.

'I want you all to know that while I am still strong, and still able to do my business, I intend to make my will. You know that I have a great many crests, which I am going to divide into three portions. The eagle crest and all that belongs to it, together with the coppers and the debts both owing to me and by me on account of it, I give to my eldest son. Heretofore you have known him by the name of Kwa-yim-gal-eese, but from now on, in all matters pertaining to our Indian customs, he will be known by the mane of Kwa-yim. He will assume all responsibility for the debts which I have contracted for this portion of my *potlatch*, and any other people or chiefs giving a *potlatch* will give him the portion that would come to me at any of these gatherings. Of course, so long as I live this portion will be mine, but if anything happens to me, it is to go to Kwa-yim. To-morrow I intend giving away the pails, dishes, crockery, etc., and I hope you will all be able to be present to receive what is coming to you. At the second meeting I will dispose of more of my property, and make more of my will in public.'

The next day, owing to the multitudinous number of articles to be given away, the clan got busy very early and carried out the pails, dishes, and glassware which were to be distributed, and laid them out in rows ready for distribution when the time should come. Two messengers were sent out, and the people were called together again. Before anything else was done, Awalaskinis stood up and addressed them again:

'I have to thank you all for coming at my request, to partake of my gifts and of my hospitality, but I feel that I must give credit and thanks to Weetsikok for what he has done. Many years ago I bargained with him through *kadzakla* for Kaakstalas, who has been my wife, and the property which I gave to Weetsikok for her has through his careful management more than trebled itself, and he has given it to me in the redemption of his daughter, and I in my turn am passing it on to you. You can see how we are keeping up with the customs of the people, and we have made ourselves unsurpassable as chiefs. I thank you all, but before sitting down I want the caller of each clan to call out the people of his own clan to come forward and receive his portion.'

The chief of each clan in turn got up and praised Awalaskinis and Weetsikok, and thanked them for their generosity and for their honesty, and the more fulsome the flattery, and the more flowery the speeches were, the larger was the gift the speaker received. Each of these speakers was given not less than ten dollars' worth of the materials which were ready to be given away. One chief of the Tanakteuks waxed so eloquent in his thanks that he was given about twenty-five dollars' worth. When the giving away of this material was completed Awalaskinis again rose, and told the people that his nephew was now taking the second ranks in all that belonged to him by right.

'You have known him heretofore as Ho-sum-tas, but from now on his name will be Kul-teet-sum. You all know that these possessions are mine to give away, and as I told you yesterday, I want to know that when I die and am gone, there will be no quarrelling or wrangling or disputes over my property. I want you all to know that these second ranks will all belong to Ho-sum-tas.'

When all the giving away for the day had been completed, the announcement was made that the next day trunks, bureaus, dancing costumes, sewing-machines, and camphorwood boxes and things of that ilk would be distributed.

Accordingly, after the people had assembled the next day and had received their portions in a similar way to that of the previous day,

Awalaskinis completed the making of his will, and announced that the rest of the ranks, crests, and debts would be given to Klalis, his son, the one who had just been initiated into the *Hamatsa*. They were further reminded that a day's rest would be given before any more giving away, after which they would be invited to the biggest feast that they had ever seen in all their lives.

The day of rest was spent by the clan of Awalaskinis in the rehearsing of a new song for the great feast, which was about to be given. This song was to tell the life-history of Awalaskinis and his family from time immemorial. It would remind the listeners that this family had been accustomed to giving feasts and selling coppers in order to feed the people, and putting coppers on the fire to feed the people, and doing various other things to help everybody else along. The song was composed by Negaiksilokw, who was the poet of the tribe, and he received in payment for it cash amounting to twenty dollars, and a pair of new blankets. The song was rehearsed several times, till the soloists were word-perfect, and they all adjourned.

The next morning fifteen hundred bags of flour were stacked, forming an arch over the roadway, and messengers were sent out calling all the people. They came in great excitement, as they knew that a lot of decisions, some of them very vexatious, would be arrived at that day, and a lot of new arrangements for future gatherings would be made. Each clan of every tribe present had had a private meeting to talk things over, and to know just what they were prepared to do in all future gatherings. The people seated themselves outside in a huge circle, and Awalaskinis's speaker stood up and called on the Kwawkewlth people to sing the song of Owhawalagaleese. The singing commenced, and while it was going on, Owhawalagaleese himself got up and started to speak:

'My father and grandfather and his forefathers before him were great chiefs. We were so great and our fires so big that our smoke would go out and cover all the country round about. This smoke going out was typical of the great gifts that we were always giving out to the people round about. I have the right to stand here before you; I have been waiting for a long time and I am intending to call for my copper as soon as the fishing season for salmon is over. You all know how much I paid for that copper—fourteen thousand blankets. Is there anybody here who is wealthy and important enough to buy my copper so that with the proceeds of it I can give a great feast and feed all the people? It is no use any little chief standing up, because, as you know, my copper is now worth a great deal more than fourteen thousand blankets.'

There being no answer for some considerable time, Negadsi, head chief of the Kwawkewlths, rose and said how pleased he was that Owhawalagaleese had made such a great speech and promised to give such a big feast that they need never be ashamed to appear either before their friends or their enemies in the future.

'This copper of Owhawalagaleese seems to be beyond the reach of any one to buy at the present time, but I want to remind you that Wanook has in his possession my copper known as Kwayimkim, and he must pay for it as soon as the fishing is over, so that I can give a big feast.'

Wanook stood up, and said he would be ready to make payment as soon as the fishing was over, and nothing would give him more pleasure or more delight, so that it would be his own, and bring great honour on him and his family, and the price of it would be a mere nothing in their estimation. He also reminded them that, as Wanook, he was the owner of a river, and that as the supplies of everything in a river were always very abundant, so supplies in his house would be very abundant, and he would be glad to call all the people together to extend his hospitality, and to share his wealth with them.

Games

Here are descriptions of two Indian games. The first is a ball game of the Yankton Sioux, described by a white trapper who lived among the plains Indians in the 1860s. The second is a Zuni Indian race, described in the 1880s by an anthropologist. Do these games serve any purpose other than recreation? Can you see any difference between the kind of descriptions given by the two white observers? Is one more useful or reliable than the other? (Stewart Culin, Games of the North American Indians, *Bureau of American Ethnology* Annual Report, XXIV *(1907), 639-40, 687-89.)*

A great noise of shouting is heard in the camp, and the young men, with bat, or club, 3 feet long and crooked at the end, go out on the prairie near the camp. Having found a smooth spot they halt, and two of the youths, by common consent, take opposite sides and pick out the players, first one and then the other, until enough are had.

One morning I heard the young men shouting for ball, and I went out with them to the playground. The two chiefs, A-ke-che-ta (Little Dog Soldier) and Ma-to-sac (White Bear), were picking sides, and a number of Indians were already seated facing each other, and bantering on the game. As each man was selected he spread down his buffalo robe and sat upon it, facing his opponent. I was selected by A-ke-che-ta, and silently took my place in the line. Presently all the young men who were to play were selected, and then several old men were appointed to act as umpires of the game. These advanced and seated themselves between the contestants, and then the warriors rose and commenced betting on the game. First one warrior advanced and threw down a robe before the old men: then a warrior from the other side came forward and laid a robe upon it: and so all bet, one against the other. Presently there was a great number of piles of stakes, some having bet moccasins, headdresses, beadwork, earrings, necklaces, bows and arrows, and even ponies. All these were carefully watched over by the old men, who noted each stake and the depositor on a stick. If you did not wish to bet with any particular warrior you laid your wager on the big pile, and instantly it was matched by the judges against some article of corresponding value from the pile of the other side. Thus I bet a hunting knife, half a pound of powder, a pair of moccasins, and a small hand mirror, which articles were appropriately matched with others by the judges. All was now in readiness for the game to begin, and the parties separated. The two lines were formed about 100 yards apart. In front of each side, 20 feet from each other, two stakes, smeared with paint, are driven firmly into the ground, and the object of the game is to drive the ball between the stakes. Whichever side shall first force the ball through the opposite stakes wins the game. The ball, made of rags and covered with buckskin, is carried to the center of the ground between the combatants and there deposited, by one of the old men, who then returns to his post. The judges then give the signal, and with loud shouts the players run to the ball, and commence knocking it to and fro with their crooked sticks. The ball is about the size of a large orange, and each party tries to prevent its coming toward their stakes. No warrior must touch the ball with his hands; but if it lies in a hole, he may push it out with his foot and then hit it with his stick.

In the game which I am telling you about, Ma-to-sac's party reached and struck the ball first, lifting it clear over our heads, and sending it far to our rear and close to our stakes. Then we all ran, and Ma-to-sac's and A-ke-che-ta's warriors fell over one another, and rapped each other on the shins with their clubs, and there was great confusion and excitement, but at length one of the party succeeded in hitting the ball, and sent it to Ma-to-sac's stakes. Thither we ran, but no one could find the ball. After much search I discovered it in a tuft of grass, and, bidding one of our men run quickly to the stakes, I hit it and drove the ball to him. Unfortunately it fell in a hole, and before our warrior could get it out and hit it, a dense crowd of Ma-to-sac's men were around the spot and in front of the stakes. The contest was violent, so much so, indeed, that no one could hit the ball, though it was continually tramped over. At length some one called out, "There it goes," and the warriors scattered in all directions, looking to see where it was; but one of Ma-to-sac's men, who had called out, stood fast, and when the crowd had scattered, I saw him attempting to conceal the ball beneath his foot. Running against him from behind with such force as to throw him on his face, before he could recover his feet I hit the ball, and, seeing all Ma-to-sac's men off their guard, with the aid of a young man, easily drove it between their stakes, only a few yards distant.

The judges at once declared the game was ours, and many and loud were the cheers sent up by our party, in token of the victory, while Ma-to-sac's men retired sullen and disappointed. I was declared the winner, and A-ke-che-ta thanked me for my services, while the young warriors gathered around and congratulated me on my success. Then we all smoked, and went over to the stakes to receive our shares. As winner I was entitled to a general share of the spoils; but I declined in favor of the young Indian who had helped me drive the ball, saying that, as he had last hit it, and actually forced it between the stakes, he was, in reality, the most deserving. This argument was loudly applauded by the old men, and the young warrior, who had not been friendly for some time with me, was so touched by my generosity that he came and thanked me, saying, frankly. "You, and not I, won the game." However, I forced the general stakes upon him, at which he was much pleased. I found that the stakes had won a saddle, half a pound of powder, 6 yards of wampum beads, and a handsomely braided knife-scabbard. When the judges had awarded all the winnings, among which were fourteen ponies, each took up his trophies and returned to the village, where for the remainder of the day the game was fought over again and again in the tepees.

THE ZUÑI RACE:

The day for the race has arrived; the runners have been up since early morning, and have taken a spin over part of the course. During the morning nearly all the members of the estufa [ceremonial chamber] drop in to tell them how much they have wagered on their success and to encourage them. About an hour before the time to start they eat a little hewe, or paper bread, soaked in water. Hewe is one of the chief breadstuffs of the Zuñis, and a good hewe-maker is in reputation throughout the tribe as a good pastry cook is among us. Hewe is made from corn batter spread with the hand on a large flat stone over a slow fire. It takes but a moment to bake it, is almost as thin as paper, very crisp, and will vary in color according to the color of the corn used. This repast of hewe is accompanied by a piece of humming-bird, as the flight of that bird is so very swift.

The runners then bathe in a solution made from a root called que-me-way. The time for the contest is at hand. The every-day attire is exchanged for the simple breech-clout. The hair is done up in a neat knot on the top of the head, and the priest pronounces a blessing as he fastens in it an arrow-point the emblem of fleetness. He then places a pinch of ashes in front of each racer, and, standing before him, holding an eagle-wing in each hand, he first touches the ashes with the tips of the wings and then brushes the racer from head to foot. Then turning to the north, he touches the wings together and says a prayer, the same to the west, south, east, the earth, and sky. I suppose the idea of the Zuñi in this to be, that as he has sent a prayer to the four points of the compass, the earth, and sky, he has cut off every possible source of misfortune and danger.

Everything being now ready, the priest leads his favorites to the course across the river. Excitement in the pueblo has reached its height: the most venturesome are offering big odds in the plaza, and now all assemble to see the start.

Should a side be at all doubtful of its success in the race, an old woman is procured to sit and pray during the entire race. She sits in the middle of the room. The racers sweep the floor around her and then pile up everything that is used about the fire, such as pokers, ladles, stirring-sticks, and even the stones used to support the pots during cooking: these are to make their opponents warm; also the mullers with which they grind the corn, and the brooms; these will make them tired. A woman is chosen rather than a man, because she is not so fleet of foot. . . .

As each side is brought to the course the priest gives a parting blessing, and the runners take their positions opposite their opponents in single file along the course. The tik-wa, or stick to be kicked, is about the size of the middle finger. That belonging to one side has its ends painted red and that of the other side its center painted red, so that they may be easily distinguished. The rear man of each file places the tik-wa across the base of his toes and sprinkles a little sacred meal upon it. Surrounding the racers will be three or four hundred mounted Indians dressed in the gayest colors. All is now ready; each rider has his eye on his favorite side, an old priest rides in advance and sprinkles sacred meal over the course, the starters kick the sticks, and the wildest excitement prevails. As each racer left his home he put into his mouth two shell beads—the one he drops as a sacrifice as he starts, the other when he has covered about one-half the course. The stick is tossed rather than kicked, and a good racer will toss it from 80 to 100 feet. Over the heads of the runners it goes and falls beyond the first man. He simply points to where it lights, and runs on. The next man tries to kick it, but should he fail to get under it he goes on, and the next man takes it. The race is not to the swift alone, although this has much to do with it. The stick can in no case be touched with anything but the foot, and should it fall into a cactus bush, a prairie-dog hole, or an arroyo much valuable time is lost in getting it out. Not infrequently it happens that one side will be several miles in advance of the other when the stick falls into some unnoticed hole. The wild and frenzied yelling which takes place as those who were behind come up and pass can only be imagined and not described. So skill in tossing it plays a prominent part. On, on they go to the southern hills, east to Ta-ai-yal-lo-ne, north to the mesas, follow these west for miles, then to the southern hills, and back again to the starting-point. The distance traversed is nearly 25 miles, and they pass over it in about two hours. Racing is indulged in by the excited horsemen as they approach the goal, and it is not unusual to see a pony drop over dead from exhaustion as they near the village. The successful runner crosses the river and runs around the heap of wagered goods near the church, then, taking up the tik-wa in his hands for the first time, he inhales, as he thinks, the spirit of the tik-wa, and thanks it for being so good to him. He then runs to his home, and, if he finds a woman awaiting him, hands the stick to her, who breathes on it twice, and he then does the same. Returning it to the woman, she places it in a basket which she has ready for it: and the next day one of the racers wraps it up with some sacred meal in a corn-husk and deposits it about 6 inches below the surface of the ground in an arroyo, where it will be washed away by the rains. Meanwhile the winners have claimed their stakes, and, should another estufa have a set of men to put up, the winners of the first race must compete with them until all have had a chance, and the great Zuñi races are over for that year.

V. RIGHT AND WRONG

Indian peoples had no written laws or constitutions of government. Nevertheless, they had to cope with the problems of keeping order and dealing with wrongdoers. How would you describe Indian forms of government—democracy, anarchy, some other term? What kinds of things were seen as crimes by Indians? What forms of punishment were administered? Were they just? What kind of personal and social conduct was seen as good and right? What role did social status play in the administration of justice? What were the social goals of Indian societies? In what ways do they differ from modern American goals? In what ways are they similar?

Government of the Teton Sioux

This description of Teton Sioux society in 1803 was written by the same French trader who described the morals of the Aricara in Chapter III. (Abel, ed., Tabeau's Narrative, *102, 104-06, 116-21.)*

The entire Sioux nation is divided first into five principal tribes, which are subdivided then under different chiefs and diverse denominations. There could be added here the Asseniboanes, their enemies, who speak the same language and have, without a doubt, the same origin. This language, by lapse of time, has undergone changes, so varied in pronunciation and in nomenclature, that a Sioux of the lakes who should visit those of the Missouri would not understand the different tribes any more than a Parisian who should visit the provinces of France would understand or be understood.

All these thirty tribes, particularly those of the Titons, yield still other divisions which are under the leadership of subordinate chiefs. These chiefs return to the rank of companions when the tribe is all reunited. If this nation had more insight and policy, it could form a chain that would render it yet more formidable to all of its neighbors than it is. But their separation and mutual remoteness, necessitated by their form of hunting which does not permit of their living together in too great numbers, divides interests and causes those of the St. Peter's River, those of the River of the Mohens, and those of the Missouri to regard each other as strangers. Then, too, the spirit of unsociability and of discord which exists among the particular tribes; the ambition and the jealousy of the too numerous chiefs; and most of all the national character, naturally brutal and fierce, cause particular enmities to arise, which not only destroy the general harmony but especially that of the various units. Individual quarrels arise which perpetuate, in families, hatred and revenge. Thus by a just defiance, which experience sanctions, a Titon is always armed even in his lodge.

Insubordination and the misuse of authority are a necessary result of this multiplicity of chiefs, who dispute with envy the shadow of power. I have known only one of them whose ascendency over the spitit of the Yinctons of the North, whom one can say that he commands, is remarkable enough to be commented upon. This savage, named Matowinkay, possesses advantages of the body, of the mind, and of the soul. At the head of two hundred and sixty lodges, which make about five hundred men, he is loved and respected by them so that they obey him blindly. His reputation and this authority so rare in the Upper Missouri gave him an extraordinary influence over strangers and especially among the Ricaras where he enjoys much more consideration than their own chiefs. A trader under his protection is safe from every insult; but, as Matowinkay never possesses anything and as his rank demands gifts, his favors are costly and some traders have paid very dear for them. I should have liked Captain Lewis to have met him on the Missouri; for I believe that, honoring him as he deserves, he would have made a very trustworthy ally.

Among the Titons the chiefs have authority only when it is a question of pillage; but, if it is a question of calming a riot, of stopping pillage, of aiding a trader in his expeditions, all authority is as nought before the opposition of a single individual.

The authority of the soldiers, especially when they are elected by an assembly, whether it be to watch over the carrying out of the laws of the *cerne* or over that of some public decision, whether relative to the store of the trader, etc. gives them the right, in the exercise of their duties, to be severe arbitrarily towards every delinquent, to kill his dogs, his horses, to break his weapons, to tear the lodges into tatters, and to seize indifferently upon all that which belongs to him. But as their right is only temporary, as they will in their turn be subject to the same sort of power and, besides, as nothing can shelter them from secret vengeance, they fear as much as they are feared and become officers of show. Nevertheless, they rise sometimes above these considerations and one of ours gave us proof of it, October 7, 1803; but, in accordance with custom, vengeance followed close.

A young man, curious to know what passed in the store, mounts upon the roof and in defiance of the order of the soldier, insists on looking, putting his face to an opening between two planks. The soldier, wasting no time in threats, draws out the ball from his pistol and fires close to the young man's face. The Savage, burnt and blinded, falls all over blood and goes back to his lodge. No one murmurs; it is the soldier's right; but there remains that of the avenger. The next day at evening, the night being very dark, Mr. Loisel's dog is wounded ten steps from the tent by an arrow which pierced him through. The soldier learns of the deed towards midnight and comes to us, armed with his pistol. He asks us to tell him the author, whose flight and the darkness had not allowed us to recognize. He departs furious, kills the first dog he meets and loads again, not wishing to end his vengeance at that. A second soldier arrives and does as much. We listen to an haranguer who cries to lay violent hands without distinction upon all the dogs of which there are perhaps a thousand in the camp. Instantly, a number of armed men leave the bushes and all the proscribed innocents would have been killed if Mr. Loisel, to avoid evil results, had not stopped the executioners by praying them to have compassion on the women, who alone would pay the penalty for an offense of which they were innocent. A roll of tobacco and the pipe calm the men.

It is necessary to remark that the soldiers belong to the tribe of the Partisan and that all the blows fell upon the dogs of Manzomani. This proves that there was less thought of avenging Mr. Loisel than of satisfying particular hatred. A poor old woman in the tumult ventured to say a word in order to save the life of her favorite dog, but a pistol having missed fire in his stomach the old woman has not harangued.

If the soldiers to whom the guard of the store is committed were honestly charged, if they really sought the interest and the safety of the trader, they would not give up even to avoid a great many difficulties. But, established under these fine appearances, they have really in view only the interest of the Savages, whom they wish to gain over by favoring them, and the gratuities of the trader, to whom they make their protection count yet more shamelessly. Such was at least the conduct of two of ours at the Isle of Cedars; for they every day exacted new pay. True they had not been elected by the French or by the nation and, as creatures of the Partisan alone, it was hardly meet for them to go contrary to his designs and his secret plans. But then they believed it made a great difference to observe neutrality and not to encourage those who complained of the trade. If they have been sometimes ranged on the side of Mr. Dorion, who is in charge of this district, it is only when their particular resentment found satisfaction and, if they have been of some use, it is because their presence impressed somewhat those who were not their friends. Apart from these circumstances, they were indifferent to everything else. Mr. Dorion escapes the tomahawk of a rogue by drawing a pistol; he is threatened with assassination by another and obliged to spend three days without going out; a man named La Rivierre escapes a gun-shot; there is a plan to kill us on leaving a feast; Mr. Dorion is insulted by the young people who often blow out his candle and throw it on the ground; the kettles, the tools, the clothes, the cash-boxes of the *engagés* are carried off every day; the pipes, the tobacco, always kept in the house by Mr. Dorion for the annoying use of the public, disappears frequently. But, in all these troubles, the soldiers are tranquil and tolerant, indicating that, if they were not accomplices, they either did not disapprove of the conduct of the offenders or dared not bring them to order.

It is seen that if things have not been actually instigated by the Bois Brulés, even to the complete pillaging of the merchandise of Mr. Loisel, it is not to the soldiers that this moderation is due and still less to the power of the chiefs. I shall not make a mistake, perhaps, in saying that we owe our safety to vanity, to politics, and to ambition.

1st. Each tribe was afraid of furnishing to the others an occasion for reproach upon its conduct in regard to the French and of being blamed for public sufferings, if they did not come after us.

2nd. A general pillage would have caused talk among all the neighbors, especially among the Yinctons whom the Bois Brulés see every spring at the rendezvous of all the Sioux, of which I shall speak later. The fear of appearing, as they say, ashamed in this general assembly was very influential in leading them to save appearances at least.

3rd. Some understood that the surest way of gaining glory and especially marks of distinction was to declare themselves in our favor. This motive awakened, a little late it is true, the ambition of one called Le coeur sans pareil (The Heart without Compare), a subordinate chief, but one of the bravest and most intelligent of the nation. This redoubtable man stations himself one day of his own accord at the door of the store and boldly declares that he is determined to die there. His known bravery causes the agitators to believe his word and everything is very quiet after that. After the camp moved, he with his family remains with us almost a month, accompanied for some time by the obstinate old soldier of whom I have spoken. They feared that some horde, evilly intentioned, would retrace its steps in order to find us at its mercy. In reality, Manzomani and one of his pretended soldiers, followed by about thirty men, had remained behind and comes with the intention of obtaining on credit twenty-four guns which we had and probably of seizing them if we refused to let them have them. But, finding us better protected than they had supposed, they tried to procure them from us voluntarily and, not succeeding, contented themselves with some packages of tobacco.

Cheyenne Law and Order

The Cheyenne Indians ranged over the plains from Montana to Colorado and were close allies of the Teton Sioux. The following selection is by George Grinnell, an ethnologist and explorer who became a close friend of the Cheyenne in the 1890s after having fought against them during the previous twenty years. Compare the tenor of his remarks with that of the preceding writer. (G. B. Grinnell, The Cheyenne Indians *(1923), I, 349-58.)*

Crime as understood by civilized people scarcely existed in the Cheyenne camp. Such a thing as theft was unknown. Sometimes it might occur that an individual rode, without permission, horses belonging to someone else. This was seldom done, but occasionally a man used the property of another, and so persistently as to cause a quarrel between himself and the owner. Such a quarrel once resulted in the death, at the hands of the owner, of the man who used the horses. On another occasion the owner of the horses, after fair warning, knocked the trespasser down with a club, and gave him a thorough beating, which ended the matter.

If a dispute serious enough to threaten real trouble took place between important men, the matter was talked about in the camp and, coming to the ears of the head men and chiefs, they discussed it, and perhaps called a council and summoned these men before it in order that their difficulty might be settled quietly. To such a council the men sent for always came. Each stated his case, and the council decided the question on its merits. Very likely they decreed that one of the men should pay something to the other. The council's decisions were usually fair and just, and were accepted by the disputants, but occasionally some headstrong man might refuse to accept the decision, and the trouble continued until a quarrel arose, and perhaps one of the men was killed. If by accident a man killed anyone in the camp—man, woman, or child—the matter came before the council, which decided how much he should pay to satisfy the relatives of the dead.

Public opinion was the law of the camp, and few were bold enough and reckless enough to fly in the face of it. Conformity to the rules of conduct established by custom and enforced by the chiefs was insisted on, and infractions were punished with a severity measured by the injury done, or likely to be done, to the community by violating these laws. As is elsewhere said, offenders often were severely whipped by the soldiers, or their property might be destroyed, their lodge-poles broken, or their horses killed.

On the whole, however, infringement of the rights of others was unusual. Once in a generation, perhaps, a man killed another in a quarrel, or in a drunken row, or in self-defense. The causes of such occurrences were often alcohol or fights about women. Sometimes one murder led to others.

The death of Walking Coyote in 1855 and the events connected with it show something of how quarrels, fights, and killings occasionally took place in the Cheyenne camp.

In the year 1854, White Horse, then chief of the Fox Soldiers, stole the wife of Walking Coyote, who was very fond of her and brooded much over the trouble. He sent word to White Horse to send back the woman, saying that if he did not do so he would kill him. No attention was paid to the message, and after a time Walking Coyote went to Yellow Wolf, who had adopted him, and said: "Father, as you know, White Horse has stolen my woman and I have sent word to him many times to send her back, but he does not do so. Now I intend to kill him, and I ask you not to interfere with my trouble, not to ask me to refrain from killing this man."

Walking Coyote knew that Yellow Wolf loved him better than he did any of his own sons and daughters, and he suspected that Yellow Wolf might ask him not to take revenge on White Horse, and if Yellow Wolf asked this, Walking Coyote felt he must obey him.

One day in the summer of 1854 Walking Coyote with War Bonnet rode up to St. Vrain's Fort (on the South Fork of Platte River in Colorado) from their camp twenty miles below. White Horse was living in a camp of Cheyennes there. Walking Coyote rode into the fort and saw White Horse and his wife—not the woman who had been stolen—sitting on a bench in the hall of the fort. When the two saw Walking Coyote, they arose and walked toward the hands' messroom, and Walking Coyote jumped off his horse and shot White Horse with his gun, the ball passing through the upper part of the chest and killing him at once. Then Walking Coyote and War Bonnet led their horses outside the gate of the fort, and sat down there, and Walking Coyote said, "If anyone has anything to say to me, I am here."

After they had sat there for a short time, Little Wolf, a cousin of Yellow Wolf, came out and said to Walking Coyote, "This is all over with; you should now go back to your camp." The two men mounted and rode to camp.

Shortly after this the woman returned to Walking Coyote's lodge. After this killing, Winnebago (*Nahk' to wun*) renewed the arrows because of the killing. A little later he stole from Walking Coyote the woman that White Horse had stolen and went up north with her.

Walking Coyote sent word to him, saying, "I am not going to kill another man for this woman, but I shall take your wife, Spirit Woman" (*A si' mon i*). Before Nahktowun returned from the North, Walking Coyote went to Nahktowun's lodge, and, entering, took Spirit Woman by the arm and said, "Come along now!" She went with him, for she feared him.

When Nahktowun returned from the North and found what had happened, he was angry, so that night he took his gun, went to the lodge of Walking Coyote, looked in at the door, saw him sitting on his bed, where he was resting after returning from the buffalo hunt, and putting the muzzle of his gun through the door he shot Walking Coyote, killing him.

Next morning he went again to Walking Coyote's lodge, took Asimoni, and made her go back to his lodge.

After the killing of Walking Coyote the arrows were renewed, perhaps by Red Moon.

One day, eight years later, in the spring of 1863, Nahktowun was sitting behind his lodge filing arrowpoints, which he had fastened into a cottonwood stick to hold them. While he was doing this Kutenim came up and began to discuss with him the question of a horse, the ownership of which had been in dispute between the two. Kutenim was a distant relative of White Horse. As Nahktowun was working away, Kutenim became more angry at him and abused him, and finally Nahktowun jumped to his feet and raising the stick which he had been using to file his arrowpoints, struck Kutenim on the head with it and knocked him down. Kutenim jumped up and ran to his lodge, which was near by, to get his rifle, while Nahktowun strung his bow and took a handful of arrows from his quiver. Presently Kutenim ran out of his lodge and fired at Nahktowun, and the ball passed close to his head. Nahktowun drew his bow and shot Kutenim in the left breast. Kutenim dropped his gun, and drawing his butcher knife, rushed at Nahktowun, who ran away, but Kutenim overtook him and slashed him on the arm, and then fell dead.

The men round about, seeing what had happened, did not go near the two. Only old women and old men ran up to them.

The Bowstring Soldiers, who then had charge of the camp, wanted to punish Nahktowun for killing Kutenim by whipping him. They consulted the chiefs, who advised them not to notice the affair at all, and nothing was done to Nahktowun.

The arrows were renewed not long afterward.

In the summer of 1864 Nahktowun was living with the Arapahoes. He had an Arapaho woman, and some people began to talk as if Rising Fire, *Ho ist o'ha a* (Smoke Rising), were trying to steal the woman. This made Rising Fire unhappy, and the more he thought of it the worse he felt, and the angrier he became toward Nahktowun. Finally he said to some of his friends, "I shall have to kill Nahktowun; he killed my cousin and now he is talking about me."

His friends replied: "You ought to do so, because if you do not kill him, he will kill you. He has already killed two men and is an outlaw, and if he feels like it he may cut your throat or shoot you."

Not long after this, Nahktowun, who was a Dog Soldier, was invited by one of the Dog Soldiers to come over and eat at his lodge. He therefore moved over from the Arapaho camp near Fort Larned on the Arkansas and camped with the Cheyennes who were on the Saline. On the day of the feast he started, with Little Robe and Good Bear, to walk to the lodge of the host. On their way they passed the lodge of Rising Fire, who was sitting inside looking out the door, and as they passed he shot Nahktowun with a gun and broke his spine. When Nahktowun fell, Little Robe and Good Bear stepped to one side, and Little Robe called out to Rising Fire, "Well, you have begun your work; now come out and finish it."

Rising Fire took an old brass-mounted horse pistol, walked over to where Nahktowun lay, and blew out his brains. *Mehhim' ik* (Eagle's Head) renewed the arrows* on the Solomon.

---

* The arrows are renewed whenever it is necessary, that is to say, whenever anyone makes a vow to renew them. This vow may be made merely as a matter of sacrifice, or it may be made for the general purification of the tribe after the killing of one of its members by a fellow tribesman, or after suicide

While certain customs and rules prevailed, there was no form of law as we understand it. There was no such thing as a legal death penalty. If a man killed a tribe fellow, he was often obliged to flee, at least for a time, for he was likely to be killed by some near relative of the dead man. If he saved himself by flight, the council considered the case, and the chief called in the relatives of the dead man and from them learned how much it would take to satisfy them for their loss. The relatives of the slayer were then called together and the penalty stated to them. When they had paid over this fine to the dead man's relatives, the slayer might return to the camp. Whether the matter was thus settled or not, the man who had done the killing was ostracized by his fellows, temporarily expelled from camp, and lost all standing in the tribe, which he never recovered. He was obliged for a time to camp away from the main tribe, and often he went away from their camp and spent a year or more with some other tribe. A common refuge for Cheyennes was the Arapaho camp, where no guilt attached to them and they were regarded as being as good as anyone else. Lapse of time might cause partial forgetfulness of the event by the people at large, but this forgetfulness never extended to the relatives of the man who had been killed. Their anger flamed hot long after all others in the camp had measurably forgotten the deed and in a sense had condoned it. Nevertheless, the slayer of a tribesman, or indeed of anyone belonging in the camp, even though he might be a member of another tribe, remained all his life a marked man.

The slayer of his fellow might not eat in the same lodge with other people, nor from their dishes, nor might he drink out of their cups. He had a special dish, a cup of his own, and if by any chance he drank from a cup not his own, the cup was often thrown away; if not,

by a male member of the tribe, or in the case of an accidental shooting within the tribe, whether the victim was a man or a woman. They were not renewed where women hung themselves, as they sometimes did when disappointed in love affairs, nor in any case of suicide where there was no spilling of blood. It was necessary to renew the arrows—in the case of death within the tribe—only where blood had been shed. This blood, as has been repeated, appears on the arrows, when they are opened and looked at, not only on the points, but also on the shafts and sometimes on the feathers. The arrows might be renewed when a man had shot himself, attempting to commit suicide, but had afterward recovered.

it was purified as stated below. No one would smoke with him. He might not receive the pipe as it was passed from hand to hand, but carried his own pipe and tobacco. If unmarried, he probably never took a wife, for no woman would consent to live with him.

If anyone had unwittingly eaten or drunk from the dish or cup that an outlaw had used, and discovered it, he performed a ceremony to purify the utensil, rubbing his right hand on the ground and then over the dish, and repeating the motions with left and right hand again until the dish had been rubbed over four times. The same ceremony was performed in case a man smoked a pipe that an outlaw had used. The stem was held down to the ground, bowl up, the hands rubbed on the earth and then passed over the stem.

It was said that his pipe did not taste or smell as it should, that he was not a fit person to smoke with. The word *ok kliwus*, meaning "one who has killed another," carried the idea of decay, putrefaction, rotting.

If people were talking and the murderer came up to join in the conversation, someone might tell him to be silent, that he should not speak. It was supposed that such a man suffered an inward decay, and would ultimately die and blow away. He was supposed to smell bad, either from this decay or from the bad dreams and thoughts that he must suffer. It was believed by some that from time to time he would vomit portions of his own dead and decaying flesh. A part of this old belief was that a man who had done this could never get close to the buffalo, because the buffalo would smell this dead or decaying flesh and would run away.

An outlaw appears actually to have lost his membership in the tribe, and the fact that he was not allowed to camp with it seems to have been a real expulsion. The man was "thrown away." True, after the gravity of the offense had been partly forgotten with the lapse of time, he might come back to the tribe, but could never recover his old standing. Not only was the man himself hopelessly disgraced, but his whole family lost caste. A young man or woman wishing to marry a daughter or a son of an outlaw was felt to have more or less disgraced his own family. It made no difference how prominent the man might have been nor how good his family, the commission of the act of bloodshed cast a stigma over his family and his relations shared in the disgrace. The matter was not only talked about and reprobated at the time, but often the blight remained on the children of the outlaw long after he was dead, and in any quarrel or dispute with other members of the tribe the disgrace was likely to be mentioned and thrown in the face of a child or relation, even when he or she was fifty or sixty years of age.

The killing of one man by another in a private quarrel was extremely rare, but there have been cases where men most eminent in the tribe did this and thereby at once lost all credit and influence. Instances of this are the cases of Porcupine Bear,—the Lame Shawnee—of Gentle Horse, and, last of all, of Old Little Wolf, the greatest of modern Cheyennes. Porcupine Bear, when he killed Little Creek, was chief of the Dog Soldiers; Gentle Horse was a brave of great influence; and Little Wolf, when he killed Starving Elk, was the fighting chief of the tribe. These men by their acts separated themselves from their offices, and became outcasts.

It was not solely the killing of a blood member of the Cheyenne tribe that was regarded as so heinous an offense; the same feeling existed if the man killed had been adopted into the tribe. There were many men in the camp, by birth Sioux, Arapaho, Ponca, or others, who had married Cheyenne women and had Cheyenne children, and who were regarded as Cheyennes. If one of these was killed, the murderer became an outlaw. Such cases were Nahktowun, the Arapaho who killed Walking Coyote, a Ponca; and Gentle Horse, who killed his brother-in-law, a Sioux. The two men killed had married among the Cheyennes and been adopted into the tribe, hence their slayers became outlaws and were treated as such.

The fact that they were outlaws justified the chiefs of the Cheyennes in not allowing Porcupine Bear and his party to count the first coup in the fight with the Kiowas and Comanches in 1838. At the time they were regarded as not being members of the tribe, and the coup was no more to be allowed to them as Cheyennes, than it would have been allowed to the member of any foreign tribe as a Cheyenne.

Those who committed these acts were often men of great bravery, whose success in war and whose standing in the tribe had made them somewhat arrogant and impatient of those who did not do as they had ordered. Such cases were those of Gentle Horse and of Little Wolf. Other men committed murder in revenge. When the crime was committed by a common man in the heat of temper, he had abundant leisure for repentance, and was often in a constant state of nervousness and alarm, fearing that he might be killed by a relative of the man he had slain.

An illustration is the case of Nahktowun who, after he had killed Walking Coyote, as before stated, fled to the Arapahoes and lived with them for some years. On one occasion, with his wife, he went out to kill a buffalo, and while in a stream valley, saw some buffalo approaching. He hastened to intercept them as they came down to water, and finally, to avoid observation, was obliged to get down very low and to creep along the ground. His wife followed close behind him. She happened to look to one side and saw, over a little ridge and close to them, the humps of some buffalo they had not seen, which had come up another way. To call Nahktowun's attention to these, she reached forward and touched him with a ramrod which she held in her hand. Nahktowun sprang to his feet with a scream, and fell backward off the bank. He said afterward that while he was approaching the buffalo, he kept thinking of how he had killed Walking Coyote and that someone was likely to shoot him, and he was very nervous and anxious. The unexpected touch, while in this mental condition, startled him so that he lost all self-control.

Small matters of dispute were settled privately, either by the parties themselves, or by their relatives. The council seldom occupied itself with private quarrels, unless they had a bearing on the general welfare. If, however, a man was worried about some small dispute, he might carry the matter to the chiefs, or to two or three of them, and ask their advice. He invited them to eat with him, stated his case, and asked their opinions as to what he should do.

It will be seen, therefore, that in the government of the tribe there was no tribal machinery for the punishment of crimes against individuals. The soldiers interfered to prevent or punish acts by individuals which were against the general welfare—which seemed to threaten the tribe as a whole; but a harmful act against a person was punished, if at all, by the injured individual or by members of his family.

The references to the killing of one tribesman by another must not lead to the inference that such occurrences happened often; indeed, they were most unusual. The first killing referred to—that by Porcupine Bear—took place in 1836-1837; and the last one—by Little Wolf—in 1879. In other words, there were only five or six such cases in more than forty years.

Crime and Punishment Among the Tlingit

The Tlingit Indians of the Alaska and British Columbia coast are different in many ways from the Plains tribes. The following description of Tlingit jurisprudence was made by an anthropologist after living among them in 1931-32. (Kalervo Oberg, "Crime and Punishment in Tlingit Society," American Anthropologist, XXXVI (1934), 145-50.)

Every Tlingit is born into one of three matrilineal phratries. He is either a Tlaienedi, a Shinkukedi, or a Nekadi. If he is a Tlaienedi, he calls himself a Raven; if a Shinkukedi, a Wolf; if a Nekadi, an Eagle.

The members of a phratry consider themselves blood relatives and prohibit marriage within the group. A phratry possesses no territory, has no property, no political unity, no chiefs. While members of a phratry perform certain types of labor and ceremonies for their opposites, it is not the phratry that acts as a unit.

What is more important to a Tlingit is the fact that he is born a member of a clan. This clan has a name denoting its place of origin, a story of its genesis, a history of its migrations.

The local division of the clan possesses definite territories for hunting and fishing, houses in the village, and has a chief or ceremonial leader. While labor, ceremonies and potlatches are performed by members of one phratry for the members of the other, it is the clan that forms the active nucleus. In practice it is a wife's clan that builds a man's house or buries him. It is a clan that invites clans of the opposite side to a potlatch. It is a clan that carries on feuds and sees that customary law is enforced.

Within the clan every person has his or her rank which is definitely known. The people of higher status, the anyeti, wield considerable power through their position and wealth, and are able to decide legal issues to their own advantage at the expense of their less important kinsmen.

In the matter of crime and punishment, the relation of the individual and the clan comes out clearly. Theoretically, crime against an individual did not exist. The loss of an individual by murder, the loss of property by theft, or shame brought to a member of a clan, were clan losses and the clan demanded an equivalent in revenge. That is to say, if a man of low rank killed a man of high rank in another clan, the murderer often went free while one of his more important kinsmen suffered death in his stead. Slight differences in status could be overcome by payments of property, but the general demand in case of murder was the life of a man of equal rank. In some instances the offending clan was of lower status and therefore none of its members could compensate for a crime committed against an important clan. It was therefore necessary to select a clan of the offender's phratry that could show some relationship to the offending clan; but in this case war usually followed, as this procedure was not legally established. In general, it made no difference whether the opposing clans were in the same phratry or in opposite phratries. Some of the bitterest feuds were between the Ganaktedi and Tluknakadi, both of the same phratry.

Thus a clan appears to be the group of greatest unity, solidarity, and integration. There was no penalty within the clan for murder, adultery, or theft. A clan punished its members by death only when shame was brought to its honor. Crimes of this nature were incest, witchcraft, marriage with a slave, and prostitution.

Murder among the Tlingit was punishable by death when committed outside the clan. The number of murders, however, was not excessive until the advent of liquor. In the old days rivalry over women and disputes about individual privileges during potlatches sometimes led to murder. Murder was generally committed in the heat of argument, and if clansmen of both sides were present, a general fight was prevented by a chief of high rank stepping between the angry clansmen with an important crest in his hand. It was considered a desecration of the emblem or crest if fighting occurred under these circumstances.

Immediately after a murder was committed spokesmen from both clans met to decide who was to die in compensation for the murder. If the murdered man happened to be of low rank and of poor reputation, a payment of goods could satisfy the injured clan. But if the murdered man was of high rank, a man of equal standing was demanded from the murderer's clan. There was generally much haggling over the rank of the murdered man and the rank of the one who was to die in compensation. These disputes always appeared in the peace dance which followed the complete settlement of the crime.

The man selected as compensation prepared to die willingly. He was given much time to prepare himself through fasting and praying. The execution took place before his house.

On the day set for the execution, the man put on all his ceremonial robes and displayed all his crests and emblems. He came out of his house, stood at the doorway, and related his history, stressing the deeds that he and his ancestors had performed. All the villagers were gathered around for this solemn occasion. He then looked across to the clan whom his death was to satisfy to observe the man who had been selected to kill him. If this man was great and honorable he would step forth gladly; but if the man was of low rank he would return to the house and wait until a man of his own rank or higher was selected to kill him. When this was done he stepped forth boldly with his spear in his hand, singing a girl's puberty song. He feigned attack but permitted himself to be killed. To die thus for the honor of one's clan was considered an act of great bravery and the body was laid out in state as that of a great warrior. His soul went to Kiwa-Kawaw, "highest heaven."

The actual murderer, if a man of great rank and wealth, often went free, but if the man was of low rank and came from a poor house he went as a slave to that house in his clan which had given up a man in compensation for the murder. If property was passed as partial payment to the murdered man's clan, the actual murderer could be handed over as a slave. Even if the murderer was not forced into slavery, his position was an uncomfortable one. There was a feeling of very close unity among clansmen and when one had brought shame to his own clan, he felt the matter keenly and for a time led a miserable life.

Among a people who divided themselves into two exogamic groups, incest was bound to be a constant occurrence and facts well bear this out. There are many known cases where a man and woman of the same phratry fell in love and lived together until found out. Songs tell of the pathetic and forelorn hopes of these forbidden lovers. The penalty for incest was death, both persons being killed by their respective clansmen. In spite of this penalty incest was common enough to make the law less rigorously enforced. In cases where the man who committed incest was of high rank, exile was imposed. The man would then go to settle among the interior people or among the Tsimshian or Haida. When the white people came with their law, the

Indians soon realized that it permitted marriage between people who were not blood relatives, and they were quick to take advantage of this when it suited their purpose. The Indians claimed that this was one of their first social customs to give way before the whites and many of the young people rejoiced at the new freedom. When an illegal marriage occurred the couple went to the white settlement for protection. A peculiar case of this nature occurred immediately after American occupation, when a famous chief of the Daklawedi clan of Kake left his wife and took a woman of his own phratry. He was too powerful to be immediately killed, and had time to flee to Wrangell, where he had the protection of American law. Later his wife died and he married a woman of the opposite phratry. He could then have returned to Kake but preferred to live in Wrangell, as he feared the stigma attached to one who marries his own "sister." At present marriage within the exogamic group is common, but in the more conservative villages marriages of this type are frowned on and the couples become outcasts.

Like murder, adultery was not punishable within the clan. If a wife committed adultery with her husband's kinsman and was caught by her husband, he would ignore the matter; but if they were caught by someone else, the wife could do one of two things. She could continue having secret relations with this man and endure the social stigma attached to this, or she could keep the man as a second husband. In this circumstance the husband could do nothing but share his wife with the other man, who often lived in the same house and was his cousin or nephew in our sense. There was, however, no marriage ceremony; but the young man was not permitted to marry another woman as long as the wife wished to keep him. This custom was common among Tlingit of high rank and the natives rationalized it as a means of keeping the idle women of the rich satisfied and at home.

Adultery, when it occurred between a woman and a man who was not of the husband's clan, was punishable by death, both guilty persons being killed by the husband. If he were fond of his wife, he might forgive her; but in this case the wive's kinsmen must pay him property to clear his honor. If the adulterer escaped, there was no way of bringing him to task except by pursuit by the husband. In case the adulterer was a man of very high rank, the husband's own clansmen paid him goods to pacify him, for demanding the life of a very high man was a serious matter. When property was given to the husband by both his wife's clan and his own clan the transaction was known as tuwatuk'ayawaci, "they wipe the shame from my face." Before reparation was paid, the husband remained indoors and came out only after a gathering had taken place at his house in which the property was transferred to him.

If a man of low rank had illicit connections with a woman of high rank the matter was very serious. First, the wive's clansmen killed two of the man's clansmen having rank between that of the man and the woman. This was to show that the wife's clan was highly insulted and incensed, and would not let the matter drop. The man's clan was then expected to offer for slaying one of its men of rank equal to that of the woman. If they would not do this, a feud might arise between the two clans which might last for a long time and might involve other clans, as in the quarrel between the Sitka and Wrangell people over a woman. In case the man's clan now offered a man, equal in rank to the woman, the woman's clan would be satisfied and would compensate the man's clan with property for the killing of the first two men. The adulterer was often handed over to the woman's side as a slave in partial payment or he became a slave to his own clan in order to compensate for the loss he brought about. During all these activities the husband remained indoors and came out only after a full settlement had been made.

If a woman of high rank became lax in her conduct and ran around with numerous men, her uncle might ask one of her brothers to kill her, which he was obliged to do. If a man of low rank had illicit connections with a girl of high rank, the father of the girl demanded either the man slain or a great deal of property. If the man was of as high a rank as the girl, her father could force them to marry. But if the girl was already promised to another man, the father was given a number of blankets.

Theoretically, stealing did not exist within the clan. Natural resources were held in common and food was but loosely guarded by the various house groups within the clan. If a man took a tool or a weapon that belonged to a member of his own clan, he was forced to return it. If a man of low rank was caught stealing from another clan, the injured clan could kill him. If he was of high rank, his own clan would make reparation by a payment of goods. If, by some chance, a man of very high rank was caught stealing, he was said to be bewitched. Then a shamanistic performance was held over him to discover the sorcerer who had forced him to steal in order to injure his social position. The sorcerer when discovered was killed and the crime thus compensated.

If anyone beside the clansmen or those invited were caught taking fish from clan territories, or if they were caught hunting there, they could be killed. This was also true if anyone trespassed on clan domain or used their trade routes. Sometimes when a powerful party came to fish on another clan's territory, the owning clan would invite the transgressors to a feast, treat them well, and give them presents. This they did to shame the aggressors, who generally withdrew after such treatment. If a man was hungry he could shoot an animal in someone else's territory, but he was forced to give the hide or pelt to the owning clan.

Adopting the crest of another clan was considered stealing, but the aggressor always claimed the right to the crest through some event in the past. Conflict over the use of crests led to war between the clans or was settled by the opinion of the phratry or the transfer of property.

The penalty for assault was payment in goods. A high ranking Tlingit was very sensitive about his appearance and if in a dispute someone struck him so as to cause marks on his face, he would remain indoors until the marks were healed and until a public payment had been made to him by the clan of his assailant. If a man of high status injured his face by falling in the street of his village, he would remain indoors until the marks had healed; then he would give a small feast to his own clan. This was to compensate his clan for the shame brought to it by his disfigurement.

If a man was injured or accidentally killed while out hunting with the members of another clan, this clan would have to compensate the dead or injured man's clan by a payment of goods. If the man killed was of very high rank and his death could be shown to be due to the carelessness of his hosts, then the dead man's clan could demand that a man of the hosts' clan be killed.

If a person was injured by a dog belonging to another clan, the owner of the dog would compensate for the injury by a payment of goods to the injured man. Harm coming to pass through another clan's property had very wide ramifications and was always settled by a payment of goods. Falling twice before a man's house would entitle the one who fell to ask for a payment of goods. Catching a chill in another man's house, injuring one's self with another man's tools, or becoming angry or irritable due to contact with others, would give a right to a small payment of goods; provided these injuries were caused by members of another clan.

Another example of this appears in the case of suicide. If it could be shown that a man had committed suicide because his wife had treated him badly, then a man of his wife's clan could be selected and killed. Therefore a Tlingit woman was very careful how she treated her husband. This punishment was also meted out to others who caused a man to commit suicide.

The Goals of the Hopi

The Hopi Indians occupy pueblo villages atop the high mesas of central Arizona. Like the Zuni, their traditional culture has survived into the present day. The following questions and answers were taken down during an anthropological study in the 1940s. (Richard D. Brandt, Hopi Ethics *(1954), 39-45.*

1. WHAT WOULD BE NICE TO HAVE HAPPEN?

B: To live a good life, to have rain, to live in plenty, no sickness, to live a long while until ready to go to sleep without pain, to have more livestock, to live with your wife without argument, to have money, to have fuel for the winter, to have dances so that we can amuse ourselves, to be a good weaver and make blankets and dresses, to have a nice patch of corn and beans, to dance, to live peaceably.

C: I wish it would rain, so we'll have crops and can eat enough to get fat. I don't care much about dances, though others might wish there were one. I wish the wind weren't blowing. [There was a high wind blowing that day.] Although the wind must be for some purpose. I wish stock reduction hadn't happened. I would just as soon it were even hotter, so the plants would grow. That there is not so much sickness. That we have all kinds of food, not so many worms and insects, no hail. That we have more money. [Would a Hopi want a pretty wife?] One woman is as good as another, but Hopi pay some attention to a woman's looks. [Would a Hopi ever wish he were the chief?] Some people might. They might electioneer for the job. But if you are the chief and don't treat the people well, your children will die. The people won't like it and will get after you with sorcery. People say the Oraibi chief has no one to light his fire for him, that is, no children. The girl who lives in his house is only adopted. [Q.] They say this is the result of witchcraft.

3. WHAT WOULD YOU FEEL PROUD OF?

A: Having plenty to eat, so I can invite my friends to eat with me. Of what I raise. Anything good—good things you get. Maybe sheep or horses. [Q.: Anything your children could do?] If they aren't lazy; you don't have to tell them, but they do it of their own will.

C: My muskmelon or watermelon patch. If I'm a boy, how fast I can run. A father is proud if his boy shoots the most rabbits on a rabbit hunt. Or if his boy learns how to carve dolls or knows how to dance. You're proud of a boy if he helps you with the sheep. Of having lots of horses. Or skill in packing a pile of wood on a burro—the way some of those fellows in Hotevilla can do it. Of a large wood pile you've brought in. Or you get something nice by working like an auto or truck; or you buy a new dress for your wife. [Q.: What would a woman be proud of?] Of her children, who are finishing school and can go out to work or get a job in the Indian Service. Or that their sons have returned from the war. Being able to cook something good. Having a nice dress.

D: A beautiful wife who can cook well and is clean. Of myself for working or being the fastest runner. [Informant is a noted Hopi runner and takes great pride in the fact.] Of possessions: not clothing [informant being very poorly clothed], but corn and other crops stored away so there is plenty to eat. Or sheep so the family can eat. Of being successful in a katcina dance, when it clouds up and rains—a result of a good heart and thoughts. The dancer himself should be meek and not think of himself as big, but we feel proud of him when the rains come. [What would make a woman proud?] Nearly the same as a man. When she knows there is plenty to live on, a full bin of flour [which she will have ground herself]. Of her husband, his being progressive. And the children. [What can they do?] They are encouraged to go out and help their father, and their mother is proud when they do. When they behave well and show they are brought up right. Of good looks and being clean. [This informant was in very poor circumstances and was the least acculturated of all informants.]

4. WHAT WOULD YOU FEEL ASHAMED OF?

A [informant was slow in starting, so a suggestion was offered]: No, not of having no money. [He is hard up. Further suggestion.] Yes, of not having any children alive. Not if you never had any. [Q.] It's the fault of Chief Tawaqwaptiwa's wife that they never had any; that just can't be helped. What shows sin is when you have children and they die. Of not being together, so that there's no rain [friction in the village]. No, not of being a poor farmer. Maybe this would be so if we had irrigation. Out here it is dry; it isn't your fault if you have no crops. Yet sometimes something is the matter with you and you get nothing. At harvest time, some have a lot and others only a little. I wonder why? Plants are a man's children; if you take care of them good, they come up all right. It's your fault if you don't take care of them. Like my son, who works for the oil company instead of caring for his crops. [Paternal pressure forced his son to give up his job, where he was earning several times the value of his labor in the traditional farm work.] A man who goes every day and cares for his plants like a baby might get something.

B: Of not having many relatives—that shows you are a *poaka*. [One of the informant's children died because he broke the rule of ceremonial continence.] [Of being caught with the girls?] That isn't so serious. [If the girls didn't want to go out with you?—this question because others said informant was not popular with the girls in his youth. Reports of the informant's dreams also show that he suffered from unpopularity with women.] No, you wouldn't be ashamed of this. But I was lucky with the girls. I never had to ask them. [Q.] No, not of being dumb. As long as you are good to people, they will like you. I *would* be ashamed of being lazy.

C [in answer to "What would a Hopi be ashamed of?"]: Being lazy, not growing more melons or corn, not helping in the work on the springs. Stealing when things are ripe. No, not of being poor. Yes, of being dirty; nowadays everyone wants to keep clean. We used to wash on a mouthful of water. As long as we were kids, we didn't care much about this in 1896. Now they go to school and know better. The old Hopi didn't have water or soap; they sometimes never washed their clothes at all. These clowns in the dance are pretty silly; I'm ashamed of them. [Informant is skeptical of Hopi ceremonial life.] Not knowing how to weave or spin. Lying in bed late when your dad is out working—but they don't care about it now. [Suggestion.] Yes, of your children not doing well at school; you want them to learn.

D: If you get caught doing something wrong. For example, about the time I was married they caught a witch, a fellow who had been going around with a drum in the middle of the night. He died of shame. [Hopi are frequently said to have died of shame.]

E: Of helping you! If I do anything bad, *kahopi*. Of not having money.

5. WHAT DO YOU WORRY ABOUT?

A: Perhaps something the children or someone else has done that is wrong. [One of the informant's children had had an illegitimate baby and had just entered a marriage her family disapproved.] Or something happens to the children. Or gophers eat off the tops of your plants. But I always try not to worry about these things. [What else?] Well, a relative dies. But then they've already gone, so there is no use worrying. Or about getting a little bigger house, but I can't afford this. [Informant was under some pressure from home to construct a larger house. Other informants remarked on the fact that he had never done so. He had once begun a house and left it about a quarter done, because, as he said, "Someone built in front of me as soon as I had started."] Or now, when there is no rain, everybody is worried about that. Or about a bad sickness, how you are to get out of it. [The informant had suffered a long and uncomfortable illness.]

B: About my boy who was killed in the war. About myself, now that I have been sick so often. About getting old. About not being able to get around very well; I'm not strong enough now to cultivate as big a field as in past years. [Q.] Oh, yes: the rain and the crops. If it doesn't rain, we won't be able to raise anything. [Informant has been fairly seriously ill the last couple of winters; he currently limps, apparently from arthritis of the knee. Hopi believe his illnesses come from his own wrong living, particularly from his supposedly having revealed secret ceremonies to white men. He is treated extremely badly by his people and by his chief, but he does not mention this.]

D: About the condition we are living in right now. About how to regain my rights. But I don't think I can; so I may as well forget about it and not worry any more. A Hopi who worries is probably thinking about his cornfield or his sheep. No grass. Will there be rain? How get it? Sometimes you can hardly go to sleep. But what's the use of worrying about it? It gets you nowhere. [It should be noted that one of the prime things a Hopi worries about is *worry itself*. He keeps telling himself that it is no use to worry, that it merely gets one upset.]

E: I wish I had children. I have nephews, but no one living with us. When I am sick, I wish I had someone to take care of me. No money; I wish I had more things. Or maybe I didn't do anything that day; in the field, or housecleaning, or making dresses, or my work on baskets. About my husband, because he doesn't come home. [Her husband was often away for several days consecutively at distant fields.] About what people say about me. [Informant was said by some Hopi to be a witch; there was also vague talk about improper sex behavior when she was younger.] And my relatives who have died. B—— is sometimes mean to me; she is stingy with the water [in the irrigated gardens].

VI. HEAVEN AND EARTH

The Indian's world was prescientific, and for most of what went on in the world around him, his only explanation was the supernatural. Consequently, the Indian lived his religion, every day. Were the religious beliefs and practices of Indians directed more toward the present life or toward the hereafter? Did men and women both participate in religious ceremonies? Was there a sexual distinction in their roles? Did individual Indians have access to their gods? Were there established religious institutions like churches or an ordained priesthood? What was the relationship of religion to healing and medicine? What was the role of tobacco in religious ceremonies? Are there any parallels between Indian religious practices and the major modern American religions?

A Crow Indian Ceremony

The Crow Indians inhabited the high plains of Wyoming and Montana. This description was recorded by Edwin Denig, a white American fur trader of the 1850s. (E. T. Denig, Five Indian Tribes of the Upper Missouri, *ed. by John C. Ewers (1961), 188-93.)*

The term "medicine men," as now used, has no reference to those who use drugs to cure diseases, but to such as are thought by the entire population to possess superhuman powers to bring about events.

Sometimes these persons are supposed to be gifted with the spirit of prophecy, or to work evil ends. This is a prevalent idea with the majority of the roving tribes and will meet with further explanation. But the Crows center *all* power in the *Tobacco Planters*. These are their own people and exhibit no outward difference either in dress or manners from their neighbors, 'tho they are believed to have control over events, seasons, the elements, animals, and all things usually attributed to the works of an over-ruling Providence. In fact they have no idea of a Supreme Being, a first cause, or of a future state. Neither do the great luminaries the sun and moon appear to them objects of much veneration, 'tho they are somewhat afraid of thunder.

This nation has from time immemorial planted tobacco. They have carefully preserved the original seed discovered with the continent, which produces leaves similar to the cultivated plant in the Western States and has something of its taste and flavor. They believe that as long as they continue to preserve the seed and have in their homes some of the blossom they will preserve their national existence. They say as soon as none is found they must pass away from the face of the earth. Several other traditions also tend to the continuation of the custom of tobacco planting. Among the first is that those who fulfill the orders of their ancestors in this respect shall be endowed with supernatural powers, to bring rain, avert pestilence, control the wind, conquer disease, make the buffalo come near their camp, and increase the number of all kinds of game, that they can in fact bring about any event not dependent upon ordinary human possibility. This is confined to the few who plant the tobacco, and who, knowing the power and standing thus to be gained, are very anxious to keep up the superstition with the ceremonies attending it. Sometimes, with a view to acquiring property, one of them will sell his right or powers to some aspiring individual. In this case the candidate gives everything he has in the world—all his horses, dresses, arms, even his lodge and household utensils—to pay for the great medicine and honor to become a Tobacco Planter. On an occasion of this kind the applicant is adopted with great ceremonies into the band of Planters. His flesh is cut and burned in large and deep furrows around the breast and along his arms, leaving for a long time dangerous and disgusting wounds difficult to heal. He is also obliged to go several days without food or water. After passing through this ordeal, he is furnished with some tobacco seed, in exchange for everything that he possesses. In this way the rite is perpetuated, and never has received the least check or interruption. On the contrary, it appears to become more honorable from being more ancient and from the difficulties attendant on becoming a conductor of the ceremony.

The customary place for the planting of the tobacco is on Wind River at the base of the mountain having this name, 'tho it is not confined to this spot alone. Other places are sometimes sought more convenient for the camp when the season arrives. At an appointed spot then the whole nation are invited to meet in a certain moon, which corresponds with about the middle of the last of April. When encamped in the vicinity the women of the camp are detailed to clear off all bushes and rubbish from a space of ground about half an acre square. Even the cleaning of this place is accompanied with the beating of drums, singing, smoking at intervals. This usually occupies the first day. On the next the spot is hoed, either with iron instruments or with the shoulder blades of buffalo. The latter is the primitive utensil. This operation consumes the greater part of the second day. The third is ushered in by loud haranguing, feasting, singing by the Planters, and all married men and women, mounted on horseback, proceed in file to the neighboring trees and cut each a faggot of wood which is tied together and carried before them on the horses. The women take precedence, and it is distinctly understood that the female who brings in the first bundle of wood must be one who has had no illicit connection with any man but her husband. If she attempts to deceive, the person who is aware of, and a participator in, her guilt steps forward and cries aloud, ''she is lame,'' or unfit for the post of honor; in which case she is forever disgraced. This has happened more than once. Indeed so rare is a virtuous woman in this nation that the above requisition has several times been nearly the cause of an entire suspension of the custom; for they would rather relinquish the whole than alter the manner in which the ceremony has been transmitted to them by their forefathers. Heretofore, however, they have succeeded in finding *one* virtuous female, or one said to be so, 'tho, as has been observed, the search has been attended with difficulty. The next important step taken in this great national solemnity is to select a man who will solemnly swear he has never slept with any of his relatives' wives more nearly akin than a brother-in-law, that tie included. This individual is found previously to their going after the wood and he brings in the second faggot. Singular as it may appear, the moral character of the males is not superior to the female part of the community, and several weeks have often been employed in the seeking and approving of a man free from the crime of incest. At one time so great was their anxiety to proceed with their custom, and so rare was the proper person that they were obliged to employ one of the gentlemen of the Fur Company to fill the office. Therefore, it may safely be conjectured that if no improvement takes place in their moral condition the rite of tobacco planting will soon be at an end. To proceed. When the two loads of wood are thus cast upon the cleared spot, all the rest follow after, one at a time laying down his burden with great solemnity, encouraged by the Planters, who are stationed round singing and drumming. Beside each of the medicine men are placed pans and bowls of cooked meat, tongues, pemmican, dried berries, and other eatables considered by them as delicacies. Those who lay down a bundle of wood go and seat themselves around these dishes and eat as much as they can. Great quantities are consumed, which have been laid up for months beforehand in anticipation of the above ceremony. When the wood is all collected, it is separated into four large piles, one of which is placed on each corner of the square patch intended for cultivation. Then these piles are all separately smoked to and invoked. Indeed, any and every movement they make during the whole performance partakes of a sacred character. The wood is then strewn equally over the surface of the place, fire put to it and burned to ashes. The whole is rehoed and threshed with willows, which serves the purpose of harrowing. Much time is employed in invocation and other ceremony over the tobacco seed, which in the end is mixed with fine earth and ashes and scattered over the garden. The place is then threshed with brush a second time for the purpose of burying the seed.

Having arrived at this point of the ceremony a grand medicine lodge next claims their attention. This is made by forming a large tent with 8 or 10 lodges connected by poles, sufficiently commodious to contain 200 or 300 persons. The interior is decked out with cloths of brilliant colors, beads, and various other ornaments. Large feasts are cooked and placed therein, and a full band of drums, rattles, bells, and whistles keep up a deafening and continual noise. Dancing goes forward after the eatables have been dispatched. These dances are conducted with strict decorum, as they, with all the rest of the ceremony, are supposed to bring about a state of happy and prosperous national affairs. Several persons on these occasions cut and scar their arms and bodies, and exert themselves in dancing without food or water for such a length of time that they are carried away in an unconscious condition from which some are with difficulty revived.

This amusement, or rather devotion, usually occupies three more days, at the end of which time they move camp and march about half a mile, the next day about a mile, the third and fourth about as much more. The idea is that they do not wish the tobacco to think they are running away from it, but are so fond of it as scarcely to have the wish to depart.

As soon as possible after the seed is sown it is desirable to have rain that the same may be washed into the earth and take root. One of the Planters then undertakes to produce rain, and by his desire merchandise and other property is collected from the band often to the amount of 2 or 3 thousand dollars. These articles are freely given to the medicine man by the rest, considering them as sacrifices to the clouds. The Tobacco Planter, after hanging up the different articles on the bushes around, commences a series of smokings and prayers to the heavens for rain. If he succeeds, the whole of the sacrifices belong to him and he acquires increase of fame. But if no rain falls, the goods are suffered to lie there, 'tho no blame is cast on the Planter, for he cunningly asserts that the time is not propitious and that some of the nation have not fulfilled their promises, etc. Occasionally he takes advantage of clouds gathering to predict rain, which would most likely fall without his aid. But they are so blind and bigoted that they actually believe in his power to produce it. One of these Planters can do anything (so they think), can make the grass grow, make buffalo plenty, and foretell any great calamity arising from disease or attacks from enemies.

When all this parade is over the camp resumes its ordinary occupations and traveling, until, about the latter end of August, it marches again to the tobacco field, when they pull the plant up and pack it into sacks. The seed is separated from the blossom and preserved; the stock and leaves are carefully stored away, only to be used on great occasions such as peacemaking with other nations, and religious rites of a national character. It is also used in extreme cases of sickness, not as a drug, but in their usual superstitious manner of smoking, believing its efficacy to consist in the article itself, rendered sacred and powerful by ceremony, and the smoke emitted through the nostrils of a Tobacco Planter.

The Sun Dance

This ceremony of the plains Indian tribes is one of the most famous religious rites in the world. The following description is in the words of Black Elk, an Oglala Sioux holy man who was born in 1863. (Joseph E. Brown, The Sacred Pipe: Black Elk's Account of the Seven Rites of the Oglala Sioux *(1953), 91-97.)*

"Behold these men, *O Wakan-Tanka,*" Kablaya prayed as he raised his right hand. "The face of the dawn will meet their faces; the coming day will suffer with them. It will be a sacred day, for You, *O Wakan-Tanka*, are present here!"

Then, just as the day-sun peeped over the horizon, the dancers all chanted in a sacred manner, and Kablaya sang one of his *wakan* songs.

> *The light of* Wakan-Tanka *is upon my people;*
> *It is making the whole earth bright.*
> *My people are now happy!*
> *All beings that move are rejoicing!*

As the men chanted, and as Kablaya sang the sacred song, they all danced, and as they danced they moved so that they were facing the south, then the west, the north, and then they stood again at the east; but this time they faced towards the sacred tree at the center.

The singing and drumming stopped, and the dancers sat at the west of the lodge, upon beds of sage which had been prepared for them. With sage the helpers rubbed all the paint off the men, and then upon their heads they placed wreaths of sage and plumes from the eagle, and the women also wore eagle feathers in their hair.

In every sun dance we wear wreaths of sage upon our heads, for it is a sign that our minds and hearts are close to *Wakan-Tanka* and His Powers, for the wreath represents the things of the heavens—the stars and planets, which are very mysterious and *wakan*.

Kablaya then told the dancers how they must paint themselves: the bodies were to be painted red from the waist up; the face, too, must be painted red, for red represents all that is sacred, especially the earth, for we should remember that it is from the earth that our bodies come, and it is to her that they return. A black circle should be painted around the face, for the circle helps us to remember *Wakan-Tanka*, who, like the circle, has no end. There is much power in the circle, as I have often said; the birds know this for they fly in a circle, and build their homes in the form of a circle; this the coyotes know also, for they live in round holes in the ground. Then a black line should be drawn from the forehead to a point between the eyes; and a line should be drawn on each cheek and on the chin, for these four lines represent the Powers of the four directions. Black stripes were painted around the wrists, the elbow, the upper part of the arm, and around the ankles. Black, you see, is the color of ignorance, and, thus, these stripes are as the bonds which tie us to the earth. You should also notice that these stripes start from the earth and go up only as far as the breasts, for this is the place where the thongs fasten into the body, and these thongs are as rays of light from *Wakan-Tanka*. Thus, when we tear ourselves away from the thongs, it is as if the spirit were liberated from our dark bodies. At this first dance all the men were painted in this manner; it is only in recent times that each dancer is painted with a different design, according to some vision which he may have had.

After all the dancers were painted, they purified themselves in the smoke of sweet grass and put on the various symbols which I have described before. The dancer who had vowed to drag the four buffalo skulls wore the form of the buffalo on his chest, and on his head he wore horns made from sage.

When all the preparations were finished, the dancers stood at the foot of the sacred tree, at the west, and, gazing up at the top of the tree, they raised their right hands and blew upon the eaglebone whistles. As they did this, Kablaya prayed.

"O Grandfather, *Wakan-Tanka*, bend down and look upon me as I raise my hand to You. You see here the faces of my people. You see the four Powers of the universe, and You have now seen us at each of these four directions. You have beheld the sacred place and the sacred center which we have fixed, and where we shall suffer. I offer all my suffering to You in behalf of the people.

"A good day has been set upon my forehead as I stand before You, and this brings me closer to You, *O Wakan-Tanka*. It is Your light which comes with the dawn of the day, and which passes through the heavens. I am standing with my feet upon Your sacred Earth. Be merciful to me, O Great Spirit, that my people may live!''

Then all the singers chanted together:

> *O* Wakan-Tanka, *be merciful to me!*
> *I am doing this that my people may live!*

The dancers all moved around to the east, looking towards the top of the sacred tree at the west, and, raising up their hands, they sang:

> *Our Grandfather,* Wakan-Tanka,
> *has given to me a path which is sacred!*

Moving now to the south, and looking towards the north, the dancers blew upon their eagle-bone whistles, as the singers chanted:

> *A buffalo is coming they say.*
> *He is here now.*
> *The Power of the buffalo is coming;*
> *It is upon us now!*

As the singers chanted this, the dancers moved around to the west, and faced the east, and all the time they blew upon their shrill eagle-bone whistles. Then they went to the north and faced the south, and, finally, they again went to the west and faced towards the east.

Then the dancers all began to cry, and Kablaya was given a long thong and two wooden pegs, and with these he went to the center, and grasping the sacred tree he cried: "*O Wakan-Tanka*, be merciful to me. I do this that my people may live."

Crying in this manner continually, Kablaya went to the north of the lodge, and from there he walked around the circle of the lodge, stopping at each of the twenty-eight lodge poles, and then returned to the north. Carrying their thongs and pegs, all the dancers then did as Kablaya had done. When they all returned to the north and faced the south, Kablaya once again went to the center and grasped the sacred tree with both hands.

As the singers and drummers increased the speed of their chanting and drumming, the helpers rushed up and, grasping Kablaya roughly, threw him on the ground. The helper then pulled up the skin of Kablaya's left breast, and through this loose skin a sharp stick was thrust; and in the same manner the right breast was pierced. The long rawhide rope had been tied at its middle, around the sacred tree, towards its top, and then the two ends of the rope were tied to the pegs in Kablaya's chest. The helpers stood Kablaya up roughly, and he blew upon his eagle-bone whistle, and leaning back upon his thongs, he danced, and continued to dance in this manner until the thongs broke loose from his flesh.

I should explain here why we use two thongs, which are really one long thong, for it is tied to the tree at its center, and also it was made from a single buffalo hide, cut in a spiral. This is to help us to remember that although there seem to be two thongs, the two are really only one; it is only the ignorant person who sees many where there is really only one. This truth of the oneness of all things we understand a little better by participating in this rite, and by offering ourselves as a sacrifice.

The second dancer then went to the center, and, grasping the sacred tree, he too cried as Kablaya had done. The helpers again rushed up and, after throwing him roughly on the ground, pierced both his breasts and both sides of his back; wooden pegs were thrust through the flesh, and to these pegs four short thongs were attached. This brave dancer was then tied at the center of four poles, so tightly that he could not move in any direction. At first he cried, not as a child from the pain, but because he knew that he was suffering for his people, and he was understanding the sacredness of having the four directions meet in his body, so that he himself was really the center. Raising his hands to heaven, and blowing upon his eagle whistle, this man danced until his thongs broke loose.

The third dancer who was to bear the four buffalo skulls then went to the center, and, after grasping the sacred tree, he was thrown on his face by the helpers, and four sticks were thrust through the flesh of his back. To these were tied the four buffalo skulls. The helpers pulled on the skulls to see that they were firmly attached, and then they gave to the dancer his eagle whistle, and upon this he blew continually as he danced. I think that you can understand that all this was very painful for him, for every time he moved the sharp horns of the skulls cut into his skin, but our men were brave in those days and did not show any signs of suffering; they were really glad to suffer if it was for the good of the people.

Friends or relatives would sometimes go to the dancers and dance beside them, giving encouragement; sometimes a young woman who liked one of the dancers would put a herb which she had been chewing into the mouth of the dancer in order to give him strength and to ease his thirst. And all this time the drumming, singing, and dancing never stopped, and above it all you could hear the shrill call of the eagle-bone whistles.

The fourth man, who had vowed to give twelve pieces of his flesh, then went and sat at the foot of the tree, holding on to it with both hands; the helpers took a bone awl and, raising up little pieces of flesh on the shoulders, cut off six small pieces from each. This flesh was left as an offering at the foot of the tree, and the man then stood up and continued dancing with the others.

In the same manner, the fifth dancer sacrificed eight pieces of his flesh; the sixth dancer gave four pieces of his flesh; and the seventh dancer sacrificed two pieces. Then, finally, the woman grasped the sacred tree, crying as she sat down, and said: "Father, *Wakan-Tanka*, in this one piece of flesh I offer myself to You and to Your heavens and to the sun, the moon, the Morning Star, the four Powers, and to everything."

They all continued to dance, and the people cheered Kablaya, telling him to pull harder upon the thongs, which he did until finally one thong broke loose, and then all the people cried *"hi ye!"* Kablaya fell, but the people helped him up, and he continued to dance until the other thong broke loose. Again he fell, but, rising, he raised both hands to heaven, and all the people cheered loudly. They then helped him to the foot of the sacred tree, where he rested on a bed of sage, and, pulling the loose flesh from his breast, where the bonds had broken loose, he placed twelve pieces of it at the foot of the tree. The medicine men put a healing herb on his wounds, and they carried him to a place in the shade where he rested for a few moments. Then, getting up, he continued to dance with the others.

Finally, the man who had been dancing for a long time with the four skulls lost two of them, and Kablaya gave the order that his skin should be cut so that the other two should break loose. But even though he was free from the four skulls, this brave man still continued to dance.

Then the man who had been dancing at the center of the four posts broke loose from two of his bonds, and Kablaya said that he, too, had had enough, and with a knife the skin was cut, so that he broke loose from the other two bonds. These two men each offered twelve pieces of their flesh to the sacred tree, and then all the men and many of the people continued to dance until the sun was nearly down.

Just before sundown, a pipe was taken to the singers and drummers as an indication that their work had been finished and that they may now smoke. Then the dancers and the keeper of the most sacred pipe sat at the west of the lodge, and the holy woman took up in her two hands the pipe which had been resting in front of her; holding the stem of the pipe up, she walked around the buffalo skull, and, standing in front of the keeper of the pipe, she prayed.

"O holy Father, have pity on me! I offer my pipe to *Wakan-Tanka*. O Grandfather, *Wakan-Tanka*, help me! I do this that my people may live, and that they may increase in a sacred manner."

The Power Vision

Visions were an important part of Indian religions. Black Elk became a holy man after the experience described below. How would you characterize his experience? (John G. Neihardt, Black Elk Speaks *(1932), 20-24, 44-47.)*

What happened after that until the summer I was nine years old is not a story. There were winters and summers, and they were good; for the Wasichus had made their iron road along the Platte and traveled there. This had cut the bison herd in two, but those that stayed in our country with us were more than could be counted, and we wandered without trouble in our land.

Now and then the voices would come back when I was out alone, like someone calling me, but what they wanted me to do I did not know. This did not happen very often, and when it did not happen, I forgot about it; for I was growing taller and was riding horses now and could shoot prairie chickens and rabbits with my bow. The boys of my people began very young to learn the ways of men, and no one taught us; we just learned by doing what we saw, and we were warriors at a time when boys now are like girls.

It was the summer when I was nine years old, and our people were moving slowly towards the Rocky Mountains. We camped one evening in a valley beside a little creek just before it ran into the Greasy Grass, and there was a man by the name of Man Hip who liked me and asked me to eat with him in his tepee.

While I was eating, a voice came and said: "It is time; now they are calling you." The voice was so loud and clear that I believed it, and I thought I would just go where it wanted me to go. So I got right up and started. As I came out of the tepee, both my thighs began to hurt me, and suddenly it was like waking from a dream, and there wasn't any voice. So I went back into the tepee, but I didn't want to eat. Man Hip looked at me in a strange way and asked me what was wrong. I told him that my legs were hurting me.

The next morning the camp moved again, and I was riding with some boys. We stopped to get a drink from a creek, and when I got off my horse, my legs crumpled under me and I could not walk. So the boys helped me up and put me on my horse; and when we camped again that evening, I was sick. The next day the camp moved on to where the different bands of our people were coming together, and I rode in a pony drag, for I was very sick. Both my legs and both my arms were swollen badly and my face was all puffed up.

When we had camped again, I was lying in our tepee and my mother and father were sitting beside me. I could see out through the opening, and there two men were coming from the clouds, headfirst like arrows slanting down, and I knew they were the same that I had seen before. Each now carried a long spear, and from the points of these a jagged lightning flashed. They came clear down to the ground this time and stood a little way off and looked at me and said: "Hurry! Come! Your Grandfathers are calling you!"

Then they turned and left the ground like arrows slanting upward from the bow. When I got up to follow, my legs did not hurt me any more and I was very light. I went outside the tepee, and yonder where the men with flaming spears were going, a little cloud was coming very fast. It came and stooped and took me and turned back to where it came from, flying fast. And when I looked down I could see my mother and my father yonder, and I felt sorry to be leaving them.

Then there was nothing but the air and the swiftness of the little cloud that bore me and those two men still leading up to where white clouds were piled like mountains on a wide blue plain, and in them thunder beings lived and leaped and flashed.

Now suddenly there was nothing but a world of cloud, and we three were there alone in the middle of a great white plain with snowy hills and mountains staring at us; and it was very still; but there were whispers.

Then the two men spoke together and they said: "Behold him, the being with four legs!"

I looked and saw a bay horse standing there, and he began to speak: "Behold me!" he said, "My life-history you shall see." Then he wheeled about to where the sun goes down, and said: "Behold them! Their history you shall know."

I looked, and there were twelve black horses yonder all abreast with necklaces of bison hoofs, and they were beautiful, but I was frightened, because their manes were lightning and there was thunder in their nostrils.

Then the bay horse wheeled to where the great white giant lives (the north) and said: "Behold!" And yonder there were twelve white horses all abreast. Their manes were flowing like a blizzard wind and from their noses came a roaring, and all about them white geese soared and circled.

Then the bay wheeled round to where the sun shines continually (the east) and bade me look; and there twelve sorrel horses, with necklaces of elk's teeth, stood abreast with eyes that glimmered like the day-break star and manes of morning light.

Then the bay wheeled once again to look upon the place where you are always facing (the south), and yonder stood twelve buckskins all abreast with horns upon their heads and manes that lived and grew like trees and grasses.

And when I had seen all these, the bay horse said: "Your Grandfathers are having a council. These shall take you; so have courage."

Then all the horses went into formation, four abreast—the blacks, the whites, the sorrels, and the buckskins—and stood behind the bay, who turned now to the west and neighed; and yonder suddenly the sky was terrible with a storm of plunging horses in all colors that shook the world with thunder, neighing back.

Now turning to the north the bay horse whinnied, and yonder all the sky roared with a mighty wind of running horses in all colors, neighing back.

And when he whinnied to the east, there too the sky was filled with glowing clouds of manes and tails of horses in all colors singing back. Then to the south he called, and it was crowded with many colored, happy horses, nickering.

Then the bay horse spoke to me again and said: "See how your horses all come dancing!" I looked, and there were horses, horses everywhere—a whole skyful of horses dancing round me.

"Make haste!" the bay horse said; and we walked together side by side, while the blacks, the whites, the sorrels, and the buckskins followed, marching four by four. . . . . .

Then I saw ahead the rainbow flaming above the tepee of the Six Grandfathers, built and roofed with cloud and sewed with thongs of lightning; and underneath it were all the wings of the air and under them the animals and men. All these were rejoicing, and thunder was like happy laughter.

As I rode in through the rainbow door, there were cheering voices from all over the universe, and I saw the Six Grandfathers sitting in a row, with their arms held toward me and their hands, palms out; and behind them in the cloud were faces thronging, without number, of the people yet to be.

"He has triumphed!" cried the six together, making thunder. And as I passed before them there, each gave again the gift that he had given me before—the cup of water and the bow and arrows, the power to make live and to destroy; the white wing of cleansing and the healing herb; the sacred pipe; the flowering stick. And each one spoke in turn from west to south, explaining what he gave as he had done before, and as each one spoke he melted down into the earth and rose again; and as each did this, I felt nearer to the earth.

Then the oldest of them all said: "Grandson, all over the universe you have seen. Now you shall go back with power to the place from whence you came, and it shall happen yonder that hundreds shall be sacred, hundreds shall be flames! Behold!''

I looked below and saw my people there, and all were well and happy except one, and he was lying like the dead—and that one was myself. Then the oldest Grandfather sang, and his song was like this:

"There is someone lying on earth in a sacred manner.
  There is someone—on earth he lies.
  In a sacred manner I have made him to walk.''

Now the tepee, built and roofed with cloud, began to sway back and forth as in a wind, and the flaming rainbow door was growing dimmer. I could hear voices of all kinds crying from outside: "Eagle Wing Stretches is coming forth! Behold him!''

When I went through the door, the face of the day of earth was appearing with the day-break star upon its forehead; and the sun leaped up and looked upon me, and I was going forth alone.

And as I walked alone, I heard the sun singing as it arose, and it sang like this:

"With visible face I am appearing.
  In a sacred manner I appear.
  For the greening earth a pleasantness I make.
  The center of the nation's hoop I have made pleasant.
  With visible face, behold me!
  The four-leggeds and two-leggeds, I have made them to walk;
  The wings of the air, I have made them to fly.
  With visible face I appear.
  My day, I have made it holy.''

When the singing stopped, I was feeling lost and very lonely. Then a Voice above me said: "Look back!'' It was a spotted eagle that was hovering over me and spoke. I looked, and where the flaming rainbow tepee, built and roofed with cloud, had been, I saw only the tall rock mountain at the center of the world.

I was all alone on a broad plain now with my feet upon the earth, alone but for the spotted eagle guarding me. I could see my people's village far ahead, and I walked very fast, for I was homesick now.

Then I saw my own tepee, and inside I saw my mother and my father bending over a sick boy that was myself. And as I entered the tepee, some one was saying: "The boy is coming to; you had better give him some water."

Then I was sitting up; and I was sad because my mother and father didn't seem to know I had been so far away.

Healing at Acoma Pueblo

The following is an anthropologist's description of the medical practices of the Acoma Indians of western New Mexico. (Leslie A. White, The Acoma Indians, *Bureau of American Ethnology An-nual Report, XLVII (1932), 107-11.)*

There are four medicine societies at Acoma, viz, the Flint (Hic-tian), Fire (H'a k'an'), KaBina, and Shiwanna ("Thundercloud") So-cieties. There are also snake medicine men, but they do not con-stitute a society; they are simply individuals who treat snake bites. Neither the Shiwanna nor the snake medicine men are of much con-sequence. They are quite unimportant so far as sickness is con-cerned, and they exert even less influence in the ceremonial and political life of the pueblo. The chief purpose of the Shiwanna So-ciety is to treat persons who have been shocked by lightning and to set broken bones. They also treat persons who have "a bad smell from the stomach" (halitosis?). It is the three societies, the Fire, Flint, and KaBina, that are really important. They cure ailments due to the machinations of witches and purge the village of these evil spirits. They also exert· a very great influence in the politico-religious life of the people.

These societies are secret organizations whose chief purpose is to combat witches. They are composed of men and women, and chil-dren who are old enough to be intrusted with secrets. The women, however, merely assist the men at ceremonies; they do not cure. A headman (naicdia, father) presides over the society; he summons them when necessary, supervises the ceremonies, etc. The Fire So-ciety has a chamber in which its meetings are held. The Flint Society usually holds its ceremonies in the head estufa, Mauharots, unless it is being occupied by the cacique, when it "rents a house somewhere else'' (almost any large room would do). KaʙIna, as we have noted before, kept his paraphernalia in an "east side room" (hak'aiya) adjoining Mauharots.

Everyone at Acoma knows, of course, that if you violate some of the simple but important rules of hygiene you will become sick; you should not eat too many green peaches. They have a number of herb medicines which they employ in treating minor ailments or complaints, and I have no doubt but that some of them possess healing properties of real merit. But if an ailment becomes serious, does not respond readily to these simple treatments, it is evident that the person in question has been stricken by a witch. It then becomes necessary to secure the services of a medicine man or a society.

There are many witches in the world, evil spirits whose sole purpose is to injure people, to make them sick. A witch may appear in a number of guises. He may come as almost any kind of animal or bird or he may appear as a person. Sometimes persons in the pueblo itself prove to be witches. There is no sign by which one may recognize a witch in the body of a dog, or an owl, or a person. This fact makes witches even more insidious and dangerous. One can detect a witch only by associating some person or animal with some malady. For the layman this association amounts to little more than mere suspicion (sometimes abetted by jealousy or dislike in the case of persons accused of witchcraft). But the medicine men are infallible. When by means of their instruments and rituals they have secured power from the animal medicine men they can see and know everything.

Witches cause disease in two ways. They shoot such things as thorns, sticks, pebbles, broken glass, rags, yarn, or snakes into some one's body, or they steal a person's heart and make off with it. In either case, of course, the patient becomes very ill and will die unless the objects are removed or the heart returned.

A person who is ill may secure treatment from a medicine society (or a single doctor) if he so desires. A sick person is not compelled to submit to treatment, but the medicine men are obligated to treat any person applying to them for aid.

Whether one doctor or an entire society is summoned depends upon the wishes of the patient (and his immediate senior kin) and upon the nature of the ailment. If the ailment is relatively slight, one doctor only may be called; if the illness is quite serious an entire society would probably be summoned.

If one medicine man is to be called, the father of the patient makes a prayer stick and prays for the health of his child. Then he places the stick in the hands of the sick one, who prays. Then the father takes the prayer stick to the doctor who has been chosen and asks him to come.

The doctor visits the patient, bringing with him two eagle plumes and a gourd rattle, and some buckskin bags of medicine. He sings, prays, and smokes. He examines the patient to determine the location of the objects which have been injected by the witch. He removes them by sucking them out, or in some cases he withdraws them with his eagle plumes. He also "whips disease away" with the plumes. He will treat the patient for four days and nights, if necessary, coming several times during the day and evening to see him. If at the end of that time the patient's condition is not much improved it is quite likely that another doctor, or an entire society, will be summoned. The doctor is paid for his services in corn meal, flour, or other commodities of value.

A patient may desire to have an entire society treat him. If he is critically ill the entire society usually comes; if the patient wishes to join the society upon recovery the whole group always comes. It happens, however, that a whole society might come with all its paraphernalia and treat a patient who had not expressed his intention of joining.

If the patient expresses a desire to join a curing society he tells his father, naming the society of his choice. The father and other relatives of the patient then make some waʙani (feather bunches). The father takes one and prays with it, asking that his child may recover from his illness. Then he places the feather bunch that he has just used in the hands of the sick child, who prays. Then the father takes the waʙani to the headman (naicᴅia) of the society and asks him to cure his child. The headman calls his doctors together, distributes the waʙani among them, and tells them about the sick child. They agree upon a time to visit the patient (they go at once if he is critically ill), after which they go out with their feather bunches and pray for their success.

At the time appointed the society comes to the house of the sick person, bringing their paraphernalia with them. A room has been cleared of furniture and placed at their disposal. They set up their altar and lay out their paraphernalia. Each doctor has a hónani (corn ear fetish) which is laid out in front of the altar. Then there are medicine bowls, small stone figures of animals, the beast gods, bear paws, large flints, a bowl of water and a gourd dipper, a refuse bowl, a rock crystal (quartz ?), etc. The medicine men are nude, except for a breechcloth. They have a black band painted across the face covering the eyes. They have their long hair tied up in front with a corn husk. Two short turkey feathers are worn at each temple.

The patient is brought in and placed on a blanket on the floor. The father or mother and perhaps one or two relatives may be there, but the general public is not admitted.

The head medicine man begins to mix the medicine (wawa). He takes a gourd dipperful of water from the water jar which he pours into the medicine bowl (waititcani), singing the while a song to the north. Then another dipperful with a song to the west, and so on through south and east. Then he fills the bowl. Perhaps he sings another song or two. Then he takes from his collection of buckskin bags some herb medicines which he sprinkles in the medicine bowl. Then the other medicine men put in their medicines. If there are any women tcaiani they put their medicines in last.

Then diagnosis and cure are begun. The headman picks up the small rock crystal which lies before the altar and peers through it at the patient. This crystal (ma caiyoyo) enables the medicine man to see the objects which have been injected into the patient's body. He can see witches, too. In fact, a doctor can see anything anywhere with the aid of this lens; even if he be blind ordinarily, he can see during curing ceremonies with the aid of this crystal. When naicꭰia (the headman of the society) has finished his examination each doctor in turn uses the crystal to inspect the patient.

All of the doctors save two go behind the altar, sit down, and begin to sing. The two remaining in front dance in front of the altar and about the patient. They hold an eagle wing feather in each hand. They move these about the patient with cutting and slashing motions (away from the patient); they are "whipping the disease away." Then they lay their eagle feathers by the altar. They go to the sick person and massage him here and there. If they succeed in finding some foreign object in his body they suck it out. They go over to the refuse bowl and spit it out in the bowl ("you can see it when it comes out of their mouth, and hear it when it falls in the bowl"). They gargle their throats, wash their hands, and go back of the altar. Two other doctors come out and repeat the process. All of the medicine men cure in this way; the headman is last. The women doctors (if there are any) merely sing; they never perform any cures.

When the curing is finished the headman gives the patient medicine from the medicine bowl. It is administered externally or internally or both. The remaining medicine is given to the members of the patient's household, who drink it.

This concludes the ceremony. The doctors go home, leaving two of their number to watch the patient. The altar, with its attendant paraphernalia, remains in place for four days, after which it is removed to the society house. The patient is attended by the doctors in turn until he recovers—or dies. The attending doctors pray and sing a great deal. If the patient recovers he will be pledged to the society effecting the cure, although he may not be initiated for a year or two thereafter. The society will receive no compensation upon the recovery of the patient, but will receive a considerable quantity of corn meal, flour, bread, etc., when he is formally initiated.

During the four days of caring the doctors may not eat salt or meat. Also, during this period, and for four days thereafter, they may not sleep with their wives, nor bathe nor wash their heads.

VII. DEATH

Beliefs and practices concerning death varied widely among Indian societies. What obligations did death place upon the relatives, friends, or tribe of the deceased? Who was responsible for funeral procedures? What were some of the beliefs concerning the existence of an afterworld? Was there a concept of heaven and hell? Did the identity of the deceased influence the kind of mourning or funeral that occurred? Did the manner of the death have an influence?

Cheyenne Mourning

The customs of the Cheyenne can be considered as typical of plains tribes. (Grinnell, The Cheyenne Indians, *II, 160-64.)*

When a man died, anyone who would undertake it, usually his close relations, men and women, sometimes assisted by a comrade or a close friend, if the man had one, prepared the body for burial. It was dressed in its finest clothing, and sometimes friends and relatives brought their own best clothing for him to be buried in. The body, extended at full length, hands at sides, was placed on robes or blankets, which were then folded closely over it, and the bundle was lashed with ropes passed many times about it. The bundle was then taken out of the lodge, lashed on a travois, and carried to the place of deposit, the immediate family following.

With the man they placed his war implements—his gun, bow and arrows, and axe and knives—and also his pipe and tobacco, and anything he especially valued. If the dead man had a bow and arrows in a cougar-skin case, this was perhaps not left with him, but might be given to his comrade or close friend, if he had one very dear to him. This was done by the relatives, even if the dead man had not mentioned it. His shield and his "medicine," which usually hung outside of the lodge, were not always deposited with him. If the dead man owned horses, his best horse was saddled and bridled, and shot near the grave. Sometimes several horses were so killed. If the body was put in a tree or on a scaffold, the horses were shot under it. This was done even though a man had killed himself, but in this case the dead man did not go to Seyan.

The spirit of the dead man found the trail where the footprints all pointed the same way, followed that to the Milky Way, and finally arrived at the camp in the stars, where he met his friends and relations and lived in the camp of the dead.

On the death of a person of some importance, an old man sang over the dead an old-time song, and prayed to the Great Spirit that created people—*Má ka ma i yó tsim ań stom ai*, "Great spirit making maker." This ceremony, still performed, is a funeral service. The song is sung and the prayer made before the dead man is taken from the lodge or house in which he lies. The ceremony is short, occupying but a few minutes.

The burial took place soon after death. Because of the fear of ghosts, dead bodies were not kept about. The dead person having become a ghost, his spirit was likely to linger near the body, and might take away with it the spirit of some person still living. This fear was felt especially as to little children. A ghost might easily take away with it the spirit of such an one, and would be likely selfishly to do so, in order to enjoy the child's society. The power to do this was believed to be especially strong so long as the body was not removed.

Relations testified to their grief by cutting off the hair. The wife, the mother, and often the sisters, cut their hair short, gashed their heads, and sometimes the calves of their legs, with knives. Sometimes they cut off a finger. Male relations did not cut their legs, but they unbraided their hair and let it hang loose.

Women gashed their legs in mourning only when some young male relative was wounded or killed in war. If his blood had been shed, they shed theirs; but if he died from sickness, they did not cut themselves. Sometimes after the death in war of a young man with many relatives, a long line of mourning women was seen marching around the camp, their legs bare and bleeding. If the young man owned a war-bonnet, the first woman might carry it; another might carry the lance; his horses might be running loose near by, some painted as for war, with tails tied up, and feathers in manes and tails.

Women did not wash the blood from their legs and faces for a long time, and sometimes went bare-legged for months. The man's relations, male and female, mourned at the grave by wailing, as did also his close friends. A wife or a daughter or mother might remain at the grave mourning for twenty-four hours. Sometimes a wife or a mother remained at the grave, mourning and refusing to eat, until her relations went out and took her forcibly away. At intervals for a considerable time, whenever they passed the grave—even if it were twenty years after the death—they cried for the dead.

Among the Northern Cheyennes it is said that persons who at the loss of a relative did not cut off the hair or gash the person, were expected to mourn—that is, to wail—for a long time; while those who cut the hair or mutilated themselves were not obliged to wail. Some people did not like to wail and escaped the duty by having their hair cut. A woman who lost a member of her family by disease showed the outward signs of mourning for at least a year.

When a man died, all his property not placed with him—and often that of his father and even of his brothers—was given away, and to people who were not his relations. As soon as his death became known, the whole camp was likely to gather near the lodge. All the relatives were crying. The widow herself, or perhaps one of her sisters, began to carry out the property within the lodge, and to throw the things down on the ground before the various people standing about who were not relations. Then the lodge was torn down and given to someone, and soon everything was gone, and the widow perhaps retained only a single blanket with which to cover herself. This distribution took place immediately after the body was removed from the lodge, and this was always as soon after death as possible.

Thus, if a man died leaving a widow and two or three growing children, they retained nothing. They went to their grandfather or uncles, and for a year or two lived about with such relatives. In the course of this time, however, some one of her relatives was very likely to have given a lodge to the widow, and she camped near a brother, who supplied her with meat; and after a time she began to get her children back, one by one, until at last all were living with her again. If she had growing boys, they learned to hunt, and assisted in supporting her and the sisters. Such a family always got along somehow. Often widows married again. A widow decided for herself whether she would marry, or whom she would marry. When a man asked a widow to marry him, she might—after stipulating for the support and good treatment of her children—tell him to give a horse to her father, or to one of her brothers, and she would marry him.

The bodies of men, women, and children were placed on scaffolds in trees, on scaffolds on poles on the prairie, on scaffolds or on beds in a lodge, and in caves or crevices in the rocks, or were placed on the ground and stones piled over them.

Sometimes, if several people died at the same time, as often happened in epidemics, or after a battle, two or three might be placed on the same scaffold in a tree.

The body of a man who died in battle, however, was left lying on the prairie, sometimes covered with a blanket, oftener not covered. Men thought it well that the wolves, coyotes, eagles, buzzards, and other animals should eat their flesh, and scatter their bodies far and wide over the prairie.

Alights On The Cloud and his companions, who were killed in the great fight with the Pawnees in 1852, were not buried, but their fragments were gathered up and left in a little low place on the prairie covered with blankets. Persons who saw Alights On The Cloud after he had been killed, state that besides being scalped, his head, hands, and feet had been cut off, and his body ripped up. It took some time to gather up the pieces of the body and put them together, but they were at last propped in place and left as mentioned.

When a Cheyenne or an Arapaho was killed wearing a war-bonnet and scalp shirt, it was considered an honorable thing to leave him untouched to be stripped by the enemy. They did not take away his fine clothing. Just what the motive was for this is doubtful; perhaps the dead man was so left in order that he might present a good appearance when the enemy reached him. On the other hand, if the young man killed in war had not taken with him his war-bonnet, or had left a good horse in the camp, these were usually given to some member of the soldier band to which the dead man belonged.

When a man wounded in battle was being transported to camp, and died on the way, they made a little house, somewhat like a sweat-lodge, and placed him in it, wrapped in blankets on a bed of white sage. The shelter was covered with grass, over which the bark of trees was laid, and over all a sheet was spread and pinned down all around.

People who sang songs of mourning for the dead were likely to sing the songs of the soldier band to which the man belonged. His father, mother, sisters, or aunts might sing these. If he was a chief, they sang songs of the chief soldier band, Wihiunutkiu. There were no words to these songs.

The older Cheyennes formerly had much to say about the new diseases introduced by white men, which were very fatal. The cholera of 1849 was perhaps more fatal to the Cheyennes than any other of these epidemics, for it is said to have killed half the tribe. When it appeared, half of the Cheyennes were camped on the Smoky Hill River, in present Kansas, and half in the Kiowa camp on the Canadian River, where the Kiowas were holding their Medicine Lodge.

Porcupine Bull, the son of White Face Bull, chief of the Oivimanah, was present at the Kiowa Medicine Lodge when the cholera broke out there. It killed a Kiowa dancer in the dance lodge; and then an Osage, sitting outside watching the dance, was struck. White Face Bull shouted to the Cheyennes to run to their camp and flee. They broke camp at once and fled north all night, reaching the Cimarron in the morning. As soon as they made camp, people began to die, among them Owl Woman, the mother of Colonel Bent's wife. Little Old Man, a very brave man, donned his war-dress, mounted his war-horse, and rode through the camp with a lance in his hand, shouting, "If I could see this thing [the cholera], if I knew where it came from, I would go there and fight it!" As he was doing this he was seized with the cramps, fell from his horse, and died in his wife's arms.

Death and the Chiricahua Apache

The Chiricahua lived in southeastern Arizona and northern Mexico. The following statements of their beliefs about death were gathered by Morris Opler in the 1930s. (M. E. Opler, An Apache Life-Way *(1941), 472-78.)*

There are no death songs for the Chiricahua. Our war songs urge the men to go forward all the time. Death wouldn't be mentioned. If a Chiricahua man heard a word about death in there during a war dance, he would stop dancing. He would go to a man with a ceremony for war and have him sing his songs and find out what it meant. Some men would back right out as soon as they heard anything like that. They'd be afraid that the fight would turn against them if that bad word was said in there.

When a person dies, his close relatives pull their good clothes off. They tie any old thing around themselves to keep themselves covered and warm. It is sometimes a month before they dress in good clothes again. Members of the family cut their hair; the women wail; the men cry.

A few minutes after death (whether a man or a woman has died) a close male relative may go out of doors and shoot off a good many cartridges in the air. He doesn't shoot in any special direction. Any male relative can do it. I don't know exactly why it is done; no one seems to be sure. But I think that this has to do with the importance of the person who has died. It tells the rest of the people that someone of standing has died. N. was a leader. When his mother died, he took a gun and shot into the air about fifteen times, right in succession. This was not done with arrows before the guns came into use. I'm pretty sure it dates from the time that guns came in. It may be connected with the shooting over the graves of dead soldiers by their comrades that the Chiricahua saw. Such shooting is not always done, but it occurs quite often.

The close relatives get the body ready for burial. A close friend might help, but it's hard to ask him. A person who lays out the corpse of a near relative does not mind so much, for he is supposed to do it, but you have a queer feeling if you lay out the body of one you are not related to. No particular relative has to do it. All those who are closely related to the dead person feel that they should help if they are called on. It can be men or women who do it. We don't like to do it, but it can't be helped. We are really a little afraid to handle bodies. Not long ago I had to handle a little baby when it died; I had to stay up and see it die. Many try to get out of it when they can.

The body is bathed, or at least the face of the dead person is always washed. The hair is combed, and red paint is put on his face to make him look nice. The dead person is dressed up in his best clothes for the burial. The burial always takes place in the day, on the same day that death occurred if possible. They bury the corpse quickly and far from the settlements—in the mountains, if they are near. They don't want children at a burial. Just a few older people who are needed go.

The best horse, the favorite horse of the dead person, is used. The dead person's robes or blankets are tied to the horse, and the horse is loaded with his belongings. His good saddle is put on the horse. Then the corpse is mounted on the horse and is held there by his relatives as the funeral procession makes its way up the canyon to the place where the burial is to be. As the funeral procession passes near the camps, the people cry for the dead man, if he was their good friend.

Out there the members of the burial party might strike a little natural depression at the bottom of a hill. They could use this as a grave. They wrap the body in a blanket or a hide, put a little brush under it and some on top, and put a few rocks on top if they are handy. Or they put down a layer of rocks, put the body on it, then brush and branches over, then leaves and dirt, and finally rocks on top until there is a small mound.

If they find a little cave or a hole in the rocks, that is used. The body is put on the floor, and the entrance is blocked up with rocks and covered with mud to hide it and make it look like the side of the cliff. They aren't going to talk about the grave and tell where it is. They don't want anyone to know or think about it.

When a cave is not handy, they might scoop out a hollow grave and bury the body in a hole in the ground. A hide or logs would be put over the body to keep out the animals.

The body is always laid with the head to the sundown. The property they brought is buried with the corpse. What they don't bury with him is burned or destroyed back home. All that a person had is destroyed. They say that whatever is thrown away with a dead person that belongs to him he carries to the underworld. They want him to have the use of these things in the other world. They don't want him to get there poor. They want to show that they do not hold property above their relative. And they don't want anything that the dead person had used a great deal to be around. It would only remind people of the one who died and bring them sorrow. Also they fear that the ghost of the person who owned the article will come back to molest the one who keeps it.

For the same reasons they kill the horse that has carried the dead person's possessions. It is stabbed in the throat or shot, at or near the grave. If a man has several horses, sometimes they kill them all; sometimes only his favorite horse or horses, the ones he actually used all the time. It is because a person used a thing continually and it is associated with him and reminds you of him that you don't want to keep it. People don't want to see his horse. Because he used to ride it so much, to have it around reminds them of the former owner. Besides they kill the horses so they will go with the dead person. The saddles are burned.

They don't have to kill all the horses of the family though. All the horses of a family are not thought of as belonging to one person, even to the man who is the head of that family. If a fmaily has five or six horses, one is considered the property of a child, another of the wife, and so on. A man might not be considered to possess more than one or two horses of his own. These are his favorites and the ones he always used, and they are killed at his death. They cut the tails and manes of horses if any are kept at the death of a man.

Everything is buried or destroyed. If a woman's baskets or pots are not buried with her, they put holes through them. Nothing is left whole, for they don't want them used again, even by mistake. Usually for a man the only things that are buried with him are his clothes and weapons. Other things are burned.

The things he used in his ceremony are not kept either. Those things are destroyed. Sometimes they put them in the grave with the dead person. Some hang them on a tree. There was one woman who died at Fort Sill. She had a cross that she used in her ceremonial work. They put it in her grave with her. Then at night something like lightning would come out of the grave.

When the person died of old age, branches of fruit-bearing trees are used to cover the grave. When an old Indian dies, they bring branches of all trees that bear fruit. They put the limbs on top of the grave. They say, ''Next season I hope there will be many of these trees.'' Young people call the dead out by name and say, ''I hope that I will also grow old.'' When a person dies in youth, his name is not called this way. When they bury a person, they brush off their own bodies with green grass and then put it on him in the form of a cross. Then they won't dream of him.

The burial doesn't take very long, and they come away as soon as they can. They keep away from that place; it is not revisited. Just witches are seen fooling around graves.

Often after a death the person who has had contact with the body purifies himself by taking "ghost medicine," throwing it on a fire, making smoke from it, and sitting before the smoke with a robe. If the smoke is plentiful, no robe is needed. He then sits or stands where the smoke can get all over him—any way so the smoke goes all over. The hair is always washed after contact with the dead, and the clothes worn are burned or thown away. Sometimes all the close relatives use the "ghost medicine."

The hair of men, women, and children is cut when a close relative dies. The hair is cut once, to about ear length, and then it is allowed to grow out again. It is done for a parent, a brother or a sister, or a husband or a wife. For a man, the wife and mother are sure to cut their hair. Some sisters do, some do not. It is seldom that cousins do it, and the relatives of a dead person's husband or wife do not do it at all. Some adults only cut the ends of the hair.

There should be no mention of a dead person. To mention the name of the dead reminds relatives of him and makes them feel bad; it only causes sorrow. Besides it might prove dangerous. To call the name of a dead person at any time is bad, and especially after dark.

We are instructed, in case it is necessary to use the name of the dead, to put a word after the name which means "who used to be called." Another way is to say "the one who used to be a relative of So-and-So." The avoidance of the name is not observed only before the relatives of the dead person. It is a general observance.

The children of the family get different names then. The person who has died has called the children by this name that is being dropped; that is why they don't want it used any more. The older people don't have their names changed because of this, however.

If you have two relatives that you call by the same relationship term and one of them dies, you don't call the other by this term for a while. You call him by his name until the dead person is forgotten. Then you can use the relationship term to him again.

What the relatives do not like if a person dies is to see in the next few days anyone wearing a red dress, a red shirt, a red headband, or red clothes of any kind. It hurts the feelings of those who have lost their relative to see this. If a death occurs near by, others take off their red clothes at once. It is because red is colorful and stands for a good time. If your relative dies and you see someone wearing red, you say, "Well, that fellow wore red when I was sad. When his relative dies, I'm going to wear red just for meanness." Fights and bad feelings can start from this; enemies can be made in this way.

For some time after the death of his wife a man will not dress in fine clothes or colors. And he won't go to social dances. He won't even be invited, because the people know he isn't thinking of such things. A woman will not attend the social dancing at a puberty rite, though it is held several months after her husband's death. She will wait about a year before she will go to such affairs.

A woman may wail for a dead relative before sunrise for years after he dies if some special calamity has come which she thinks wouldn't have come if the relative were alive. Or she may wail when she sees a special friend of her dead son, or one who is of the same age and looks like him.

Our concept is down, a place beneath. When I was a child, many years ago, the Chiricahua never talked about where other Indians go at death. They just talked about where their own people, the Chiricahua, go. We think of a dead person going on to another life—of his whole body, as it was on earth, going to the other world. He is really transferred to that other world.

When a person is very sick and unconscious, it is said that he is somewhere else, that his ghost has gone where the dead people are, to visit his friends. If he regains consciousness, it is because his ghost gets back again, and when he gets well he may tell where he was. Every once in a while someone has an experience like this. That is how we know where the place is and what it looks like.

For instance, when I was a little boy someone was very sick, more dead than alive. He peeped into the underworld. But he didn't quite go there. He came back and told what he saw. He described the entrance to it as a huge sand pile upon which people are dropped and which they are trying to climb. But the sand gives way, and they don't get to this world again. The underworld, according to this man, lies just below our present world.

When a person dies, he goes under the ground. He goes through an opening in the ground which is cut out like a window. Someone leads him to it so he can't miss it. There is tall grass all around it to hide it and make it look natural. When this opens, there is a great pile of sand, shaped like a tepee or cone, stretching down beneath. It is a far distance from the top to the bottom. Once a person is down there, it is almost impossible to get back. Once he is through the gate it is impossible for the person who is really dead to come back to life; yet some who are just very sick or in a death coma, but who later recover, can come back and tell about it. This big sand hill closes off the underworld for those who are there. If you are in the underworld and succeed in getting to the top of it, you will get back to earth and life. But it is almost impossible. Many try it. They get up so far, and then the sand rolls down with them.

The same ways we have here are carried on down there too. Those people dance, eat, and sleep. A person down there can actually feel another in the flesh. The people remain the same age as they were when they died. I saw people as they were when they went. That is the way it is always seen. There is no sickness, death, pain, or sorrow there. Those who were good and those who were bad are down there together. I saw them all mixed together. The same places, the same sacred mountains, the same ceremonies exist there as here. It is just as though everything is transferred to a different country.

There is no death there, but lots of good things to eat. Affairs go on in the same way, but better. Those who are there just go on living happily. Life means more. It is always the same life, the hunting, the raids, and all, as in the old days. There are the same puberty rite, masked dances, and sacred mountains. In the underworld they are just like a big community, but they are split up into the same groups as on earth. Each person is with his own group. And each does the same things he used to do when he was on earth. As the story goes, if you were an arrow-maker, you are there making arrows. If you were a good hunter, you are over there hunting. If you were a great warrior on earth, you are out at war.

Death Among the Potlatch People

The potlatch described in Chapter IV had an unexpected result. (Halliday, Potlatch and Totem, *108, 111-18.)*

Negai then held a conference with Tatanseet, who was the second chief of the eagles, and they decided on a plan of campaign. Each of them now knew just how far the other was prepared to go, so that they might humble Awalaskinis to the dust. They knew that with all the giving away he had done, his credit was strained to the utmost, and they knew from the lavish gifts he had given that he could have very little left, so they did not anticipate any great trouble in humiliating him, so that for years he would not be able to lift up his head again in honour at any of the *potlatch* gatherings.

When all their arrangements were complete, they sent messengers round again calling the people to a gathering out of doors. It was getting well on to the spring and the days were balmy and pleasant, and it allowed more room for a large crowd so that they might stage their reprisals against Awalaskinis.

Tatanseet, whose rank had been usurped by Awalaskinis, then got up and addressed the crowd:

'My father and his forefathers before him have always been very generous. They have given away wealth beyond what one is able to count. They have always been honest people. They have always been straight in their dealings. What they had they got by their own merits. Now comes along this upstart who calls himself Awalaskinis, and simply because he has been able to give away a few blankets and a few other things, thinks he can step into my shoes and take my rank away from me in the eagle clan. I never heard of such presumption in my life, and I have joined forces with Negai to show Awalaskinis that he is only an upstart and that all the wealth he ever had he got by fraud, and had it not been for the generosity of Weetsikok in the redemption of his daughter, he would never have been able to give away the amount that he did, and the glory that he gets from that is only second-hand, it is due to the generosity of Weetsikok. Now I own three coppers which are bought and paid for; I don't owe a cent on them; I am going to destroy these coppers and hurl them with my defiance at the head of Awalaskinis.'

The same three chiefs who had cut up the other coppers for Negai then proceeded to cut up the three coppers of Tatanseet who, instead of acting in the usual way by sending a messenger to Awalaskinis with the broken pieces, walked over to where Awalaskinis sat and threw the pieces straight in his face, saying: 'You have my defiance now. Do your worst!'

Awalaskinis rose to his feet, took his speaker's staff, and was so enraged over what had been done that he started a very impassioned speech. He hurled abuse at Negai; he hurled abuse at Tatanseet; he called them both cowards, liars, thieves, and other vile names, finally working himself into such a rage that he was foaming at the mouth. Suddenly he put his hand up to his head and fell to the ground in a state of collapse. He was carried away by some of his young men to his own house, and put into his bed, while the meeting without his presence fell very flat; but the custom demanded that the usual giving away must not be overlooked, the people expected it and that was what they had come for. Negai called the speaker of his clan to him and instructed him to see that every person present received one dollar in silver; he was a great chief and it was necessary that he should be very generous.

Tatanseet then distributed in the usual way fifty cents in silver to each person present, and they all dispersed for the day and would be prepared to be called on when Awalaskinis recovered from what they thought was only a passing faintness. They did not realize at the time that the shock together with the terrible rage into which Awalaskinis had thrown himself would have a serious after-effect.

Awalaskinis had no wife to care for him, but he had one sister left, and she sat by him; but before midnight the call came for him, and he breathed his last, and went to render his account to his Creator. As soon as the breath was out of his body, the sister commenced to cry and wail, and scratched her face with both hands till the blood poured down her cheeks. When the wail was heard by those in the near vicinity, the members of his clan took it up, till the sound could be heard for miles. One of the young men said: 'We must prepare him for burial,' so a large trunk with leather straps was brought in, and the body of Awalaskinis was doubled up to fit it. As the body was rather large, the lid of the trunk did not close properly, so one of the young men stood on the shoulders of the corpse and forced it into such a position that the lid could be shut. The trunk was then securely locked and fastened. The wailing continued all night, and early the next morning all the people were notified by messenger to prepare to lay the body away.

When breakfast was over, the people in the village gathered in front of the house of Awalaskinis to show sympathy for the living relatives and also to show their respect for the dead chief. When all were assembled, Negadsi, the head chief for the whole assembly, stood up and addressed the people:

'Friends, chiefs, and nobles! We are all gathered together here to-day to lay away to his last rest one who has been with us for so many years. The shock of his sudden death is very great to us all. We had thought that he would be with us for many more years, and that he would be able to continue to add to the many laurels which he has already gathered, but this was not to be. We want to show our sympathy for the sister and the sons of Awalaskinis, and try to strengthen them in their sorrow. We know that the great chief who has just died has given one of the greatest *potlatches* that have ever been given amongst our people. This must be a matter of great rejoicing to his friends and relatives. Now to these friends and relatives I would say that it is your duty to uphold the ranks which you have inherited. Never forget that you are a great family; you must pull yourselves together and show yourselves as great as your father was. We shall all expect you to continue the same old customs and to be generous in the gifts you give away to your friends. We shall all mourn for the great chief, but we must remember that your forefathers all passed away and the people mourned for them; and so do we for Awalaskinis. I hope all the people present will encourage the rest of his family and help them along on their way.'

The rest of the chiefs followed according to rank and precedence; soon it came to Negai's turn to speak, and he said:

'Awalaskinis has passed and gone, and it would be out of place for me to-day to say anything against him. However, it is impossible for me to forget that amongst his last acts he hurled defiance at me and at my friends. I in my turn have hurled my defiance at him, but knowing the old custom is not yet completed, I will await their good pleasure to have everything completed at a later date.'

When all the chiefs had finished speaking, the speaker of Awalaskinis's clan got up and said: 'I, with all the rest of his friends, am mourning for the great chief who has gone away. We will take him away and lay his body very carefully in the place that has been prepared for it, and I am very glad to see you all here. Kwa-yim, you will remember, was made heir to the first of his crests, and he will give away to-day five hundred dollars in cash; and I would ask all the singers to get their mourning songs ready, and we will get new ones specially prepared for our great chief who has passed away. At the present time we are not thinking of what Negai and Tatanseet have done, but we will take that up later. The great name of Awalaskinis will never fail; the name of his clan will never fail; we are great at doing everything and we are very hard to fight against.'

When the speaking was over, the trunk containing the body was carried away to some distance, where the stump of a huge tree which had been sawed off remained standing, and the trunk containing the body was laid on the top of the stump and covered over temporarily with huge button blankets. The following morning a wooden house was erected over the top of the box, and the figure of a great whale, which was the principal crest the right to which had not been disputed, was painted on the side of the house, and all the other crests belonging to him were shown on the various walls of the house. Each artist who had assisted in the work received liberal payment for his efforts.

The morning after the funeral the clan cleaned up the house of the late chief, and burned all his clothing, blankets, beds, mattresses, besides the furniture which had been in common use. Then the singers came into the house and rehearsed four new songs which they intended to sing on the following day about the greatness of Awalaskinis from the time of his forefathers up to the present. Apparently the songs pleased the speaker of the clan, and they were thanked for their trouble, but they replied that it would take four days to complete the rehearsals, but in that time they expected to be ready to sing the praises publicly. The rehearsals were continued for the four days, after each one of the singers was fed by the sister of Awalaskinis on the usual Indian food of dried salmon and oolachan grease.

On the fourth day Kwa-yim called every one together by means of the heralds, and when they had all assembled, he informed them through the speaker that the sister intended giving away first to all the women; accordingly they were all presented with various articles of clothing: jerseys, silk shawls, shoes, and other things which she had been able to accumulate.

Then Kwa-yim paid everybody who had taken any part in the funeral; those who had assisted in the composing of or singing the songs were given ten dollars in cash, and the others who had taken part in other ways received five dollars each in cash and a blanket. When this was done, the singers were called on to sing the new songs. The men in the assembly were all at one end near the back of the house, and the women stood side by side in the room in a double line. Kwa-yim selected four of the closest family relatives of Awalaskinis to be the chief mourners at this gathering, and they stood on a bench in front near the fire. While the songs were being sung, these four swayed their bodies backward and forward, keeping time to the music, keeping up a low wail, and continued scratching their faces till the blood ran down and dropped on their shoulders. When the fourth song was completed, the sound of a horn was heard at the rear of the building, and when the horn stopped they heard a *hamatsa* whistle. The speaker of Awalaskinis's clan got up and told the people that their great chief's spirit had come back, and asked the other chiefs present to go out and bring it in, as it was waiting outside. Obedient to the request, the men went outside and returned, bringing with them a masked figure dressed as a *hamatsa*, but instead of having the bearskin robe, there was a button blanket wrapped round him, and a huge false face to hide his own features. This false face had a very large open mouth, and was painted a bright red. One of the chiefs spoke and said: 'We have brought back your chief with his great crests as you have often seen him.' Blankets were spread all round, and the masked figure walked round the room, very slowly, on top of the blankets, and as he went out at the back door he threw off the red cedar-bark girdle and head-dress which he had worn, along with the mask, and they heard one faint *hamatsa* whistle, which seemed to come a long distance.

The speaker then rose again, and said: 'I am very glad that we have been able to see our great chief once more, and I will now take this cedar bark which he left behind him as a memento and I will put it away carefully amongst his other effects. Every time there is a *potlatch* given by Kwa-yim or Klalis, when they are able to give away, this memento will be brought out so that we can realize that the spirit of Awalaskinis is still with us.'

Kwa-yim then got up and said: 'My father, when he was alive, broke a copper; but you will notice that in the breaking of it he left the cross, which is the heart of the copper, intact. I want you all to bear witness that as soon as I am old enough I will do as my father did, and will give away to all the people. In the meantime I am giving the heart of this copper to Negai. You all know what this means: that I will carry on the enmity which my father and Negai engendered during their lives. My father was called away before he had an opportunity to fight this matter to a finish, but I intend to carry on the same as he has done.'

According to the Indian custom, it was compulsory for Negai to accept the heart of the copper or he would be forever disgraced, so he made the best of the situation and accepted it, and thanked Kwa-yim for what he had done, because it showed that he had the old custom still at heart, but he must remember that for the time being he (that is, Negai) was the master of the situation.

Kwa-yim then replied: 'We will now for ever put away the name of Awalaskinis; our hearts are all very sore. Still I am his son, and as you will remember, a few days ago he changed my name of Kwa-yim-gal-eese, by which you have known me since I was a boy, to Kwa-yim, and in future I will refuse to acknowledge any other name.'

The chiefs who were present in turn spoke, congratulating Kwa-yim on the stand he had taken, and before they left the building every one present had received money, two dollars for each chief, a dollar for each man, and fifty cents for each woman.